KT-447-687

Pet Owner's Guide to

THE LABRADOR RETRIEVER

Diana Beckett

RINGPRESS

Published by Ringpress Books,
Vincent Lane, Dorking, Surrey,
RH4 3YX, England.

First Published 1994
This edition reprinted 1998

ISBN 0 948955 93 7

Printed and bound in Hong Kong by Printworks International

Contents

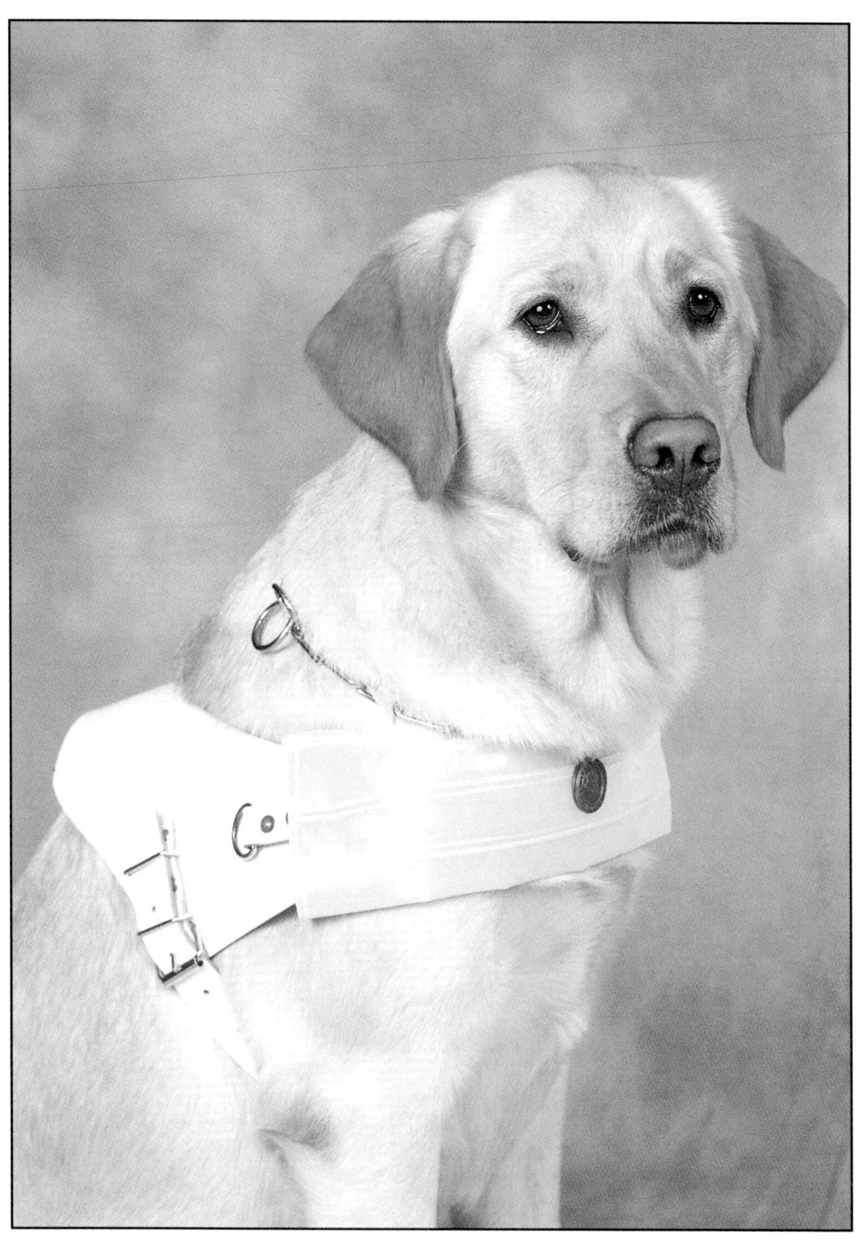

Gentle, calm and intelligent, the Labrador Retriever is used as a guide dog for the blind all over the world.

Author Diana Beckett with Kimvalley Drummer.

About the author

Diana Beckett has owned Labradors since her early teens, and she has bred and exhibited the breed for the last thirty-five years. She managed a large show kennel in America for several years, and during this time she made up fifteen American Champions. She has made up four home-bred Champions, as well having Champions in Germany and Denmark. Her stock is well-known in the show ring, and in working kennels. Diana is an International Championship Show judge, and she has been to the USA, Sweden, Finland, Denmark, Holland, France, and Germany on judging appointments. In 1990 she judged the breed at Crufts.

Acknowledgements

Thanks to the Guide Dogs for the Blind Association and the Metropolition Police for the use of photographs.

Photography by Carol Ann Johnson.

Chapter One

ORIGINS OF THE LABRADOR

THE FISHERMAN'S DOG

Many theories have been put forward as to the origins of the Labrador, and it is sometimes difficult to separate fact from fiction. However, the breed has always attracted thoughtful and diligent breeders, who have kept detailed records, and this has proved to be a tremendous bonus in the development of the Labrador.

The history of the breed can be traced back to Newfoundland, a bleak, inhospitable region of Canada, discovered by John Cabot in the fifteenth century, although archaeological discoveries have located Viking settlements dating back to at least AD 1000. However, when John Cabot set foot on Newfoundland, he discovered that nobody lived there. The Vikings had left, Indians had been and gone, and Eskimos, a race well-known for working with dogs, had also left the region. No traces of dogs were found, but in later years archaeologists did find remains of a large dog, which could possibly have been the forerunner of the Newfoundland Dog. This could have been a companion of the early Indian settlers; its size would have made it an ideal member of any tribe. It could have carried packs, pulled sleds, or may have been used as a huge hot-water bottle for children.

John Cabot was swift to discover the fishing potential of Newfoundland, and soon the English fishing fleet was at work off the coasts. This was around 1450-1458. The fleet owners were hard taskmasters, and they were ever mindful of competition. Fishermen were forbidden to settle on the islands, in case they got ideas of setting up their own industry. But settle they did, in spite of a law forbidding settlement within six miles of the coast. It was a hard, rough life, and the fishermen, who were mostly from Devon and Dorset, were a tough, hard-bitten lot. They were illiterate to a man, but wise in all manner of country pursuits, including the capture of game for the pot.

They probably had dogs at home who retrieved birds or rabbits from right under the gamekeepers' noses, and these four-legged partners in crime were sorely missed when it came to finding food in a foreign land. Now comes the all-important question: did they take their dogs on the boats with them from England, or did they find a dog that could be trained as a helpmate in this new country?

It is documented that the Devon and Dorset fishermen in those days fished from off the Newfoundland coast in a boat known as a dory – an open boat, rowed with heavy sweeps or oars. They invariably had a dog on board, which was smaller than a Newfoundland, with a shorter, denser coat, and a willingness to enter the icy waters to retrieve fish that escaped from the nets. I believe that the dogs who swam out to the nets must have been been the larger 'Newfoundland' type dog, as towing a fishing net weighing hundreds of pounds, even in a moderate sea, would call for a dog the size of a Shetland pony. The smaller type of dog had many of the same attributes, namely a willingness to work in water, and a coat that shed water quickly and was so dense that the dog could withstand the icy conditions. These dogs would have to be hauled back into the boats by the scruff of the neck when the work was over.

These were the two types of dogs that went into the interior with the early settlers in the sixteenth century. By the early 1800s both types were found in the St. John's area of Newfoundland. One, a heavy-coated, large, black animal was used not only for swimming out with the nets but also as a draught dog, pulling the sleds full of dried fish. The other, a smaller dense-coated dog, was adept at retrieving on land and water. We can only speculate as to whether the smaller dog came over from England. It could have been a cross from the English St. Hubert Hound.

THE SHOOTING COMPANION

The continuous trade between Newfoundland and England meant that the St. John's Dog, with a reputation as a retriever second to none, was soon noticed by English sportsmen. This was the age when the English gentry lived in huge country houses with large estates. The popular pastime was shooting, and the English aristocracy were determined to own the very best gundogs.

The second Earl of Malmesbury lived near Poole in Dorset, which was one of the principal ports in the Newfoundland fishing trade. Lord Malmesbury and Colonel Peter Hawker bought several dogs from the fishermen. In fact, it was Colonel Hawker who, around 1812, gave names to the two types of dog. The larger dog became known as the Newfoundland, and the smaller dog was known as the lesser Newfoundland, the Labrador, or St. John's Dog. Colonel Hawker wrote a book in 1814 called *Instruction To Young Sportsmen*, in which he described the Labrador as "by far the best dog for every kind of shooting".

It was not long before the Labrador's reputation became more widespread, and the Duke of Buccleuch, Lord Home, the Hon. Arthur Holland-Hibbert (later to become Lord Knutsford) joined the band of Labrador owners. They were an informed group of fanciers, and fortunately for us, they bred true to type, and kept records of their dogs' pedigrees. The Hon. Arthur Holland-Hibbert was particularly noted for producing good, sound dogs, and his strain was given the kennel name of Munden. In fact, it was a dog called Munden Single who, in 1904, became the first Labrador to run in a field trial. In the same year Labradors were listed a separate breed by the Kennel Club, and the seven registered were all owned by the Munden kennel.

The Earl of Verulam was one of the early owners and breeders of Labradors, and he owned a dog called Sweep. In later years, after the Second World War, my father was chauffeur to the then Earl of Verulam. At his Hertfordshire home, Gorhambury, there was a black Labrador, also named Sweep, and it was seeing this dog – a first-class worker, with the most lovely expression – that started my love for the breed.

INFLUENTIAL DOGS

Buccleuch Avon was one of the earliest important dogs, and he was probably the ancestor of all black Labradors. Avon, who was sired by Malmesbury Tramp out of a bitch called June, was bred by Lord Malmesbury in 1885. He was given to the Duke

The Labrador Retriever was first used as a fisherman's dog. Most Labradors are excellent swimmers, and their coat is ideal for shedding water quickly.

The family favourite: The Labrador Retriever is one of the most popular and best-loved of companion dogs.

The gundog par excellence: The Labrador's athletic build, biddable temperament and excellent sense of smell make it the perfect shooting companion.

of Buccleuch along with two Labradors, namely Ned and Nell. Avon was reported to have been a lovely dog, with a splendid head and the kindest of expressions. It has been stated that his birth was the most important date in the history of the Labrador.

The other famous dog of this early time was Nell, owned by the 11th Earl of Howes. Looking at photographs of Nell, she also seems to have had a good head, with a lovely, kind expression. She also had four white feet but, because of the careful breeding this fault was eliminated, and we have the whole coloured dog known today as the Labrador Retriever.

THE VERSATILE LABRADOR

Since those early days, the Labrador Retriever has excelled in many roles. It remains a gundog par excellence; it is among the most popular breeds to be used as guide dogs for the blind, and its tremendous sense of smell makes it ideal as a sniffer dog, employed by the security forces in arms and drug detection. Most important of all, the Labrador's outstanding temperament, marked by its willingness to please, makes the breed one of the world's most popular and best-loved family pets.

Chapter Two

CHOOSING A PUPPY

Now that you have decided to own a dog, and you have chosen the Labrador Retriever as the breed you want, it is worthwhile spending a little time on choosing the right puppy. Remember, this is to be your companion and your family's companion for, hopefully, the next ten years or more.

A DOG TO SUIT YOUR LIFESTYLE

If you have a young family, or you plan to have children, I think it is a good idea to have a puppy to grow up with them – providing you give the pup the attention he deserves, or has got used to prior to the advent of a baby. As children grow older and more mobile, do not allow them to poke and pull at a puppy or at an an older dog. Children must learn to respect animals. I always said to my children: "If you torment the dogs and they bite you, it will be *you* I shall punish." I now hear my children giving the same lesson to *their* children, and I believe it is essential for all dog owners with children to establish a mutual understanding.

Generally, Labradors seem to have a great affinity with children. Toddlers are the right size to be used as pillows on the floor, or a constant supplier of food. As the children get older, they become playmates – someone who will throw a ball or take the dog on exciting walks. A certain affection, perhaps you could call it devotion, seems to develop between a child and a puppy who grow up together. Of course, older dogs give the same love and affection, but I think that there is a greater sense of achievement when you have reared your Labrador from puppyhood and it has grown into the adult dog that you want.

There are drawbacks to taking on a Labrador puppy that you should be aware of. The puppy will miss his mother and brothers and sisters, and the first few nights may be sleepless, for all concerned. The pup will need to be house trained – you cannot expect a pup to be house trained overnight – and there will also be the teething stage when the pup chews everything in sight, including the furniture.

THE OLDER DOG

If you are going to be away during the day for long periods of time, such as being out at work, then it may be a better idea to acquire an older dog, who has already been taught some manners. This also applies if you are older, and you do not want to take the chance of being tripped up or knocked down by a boisterous pup. Many breeders, myself included, have older kennel dogs that they would like to put into a home where they can become a much-loved family pet, occupying the number one spot on the hearth-rug, instead of living in a kennel for the rest of their lives.

A special bond develops between a child and a dog if they grow up together.

The chocolate Labrador Retriever is the most difficult colour to breed, and the colour can be affected by exposure to sunshine.

The choice of colour is a matter of personal preference – all are equally appealing. The yellow Labrador can range from light cream to red-fox.

There are many reasons why older dogs become available from breeders. It could be that the dog has been retained as a potential show dog, only to find that it is not up to show standard, or it may be that the dog dislikes showing, and in this instance a dog will rarely be successful. There are also bitches who have grown too old to be bred from, or a stud dog who is no longer to be used for this purpose. These kennel dogs have usually been lead and car trained and, as most of them have been self-taught to be clean in their kennels, they adapt very quickly to being clean in a house. The other way to obtain an older dog is through a Labrador Retriever Rescue Scheme.

DOG OR BITCH

If you are buying a puppy with a view to getting involved in breeding Labradors – having done all your homework on why you want to become a breeder – then you must begin with a bitch, and she must be the very best in every way that you can afford. The reason for this is simple: unless you are lucky enough to obtain a male who is very successful in the show ring or is an excellent worker, you are unlikely to have many requests for matings. Even if you do, you will not be the breeder of the resulting offspring. So, to start off your career in breeding, a good foundation bitch is essential.

If you are buying your puppy purely as a companion, it is a matter of personal choice whether you want a dog or a bitch. However, do not let people tell you that males are not so loving, or so easy to train as females. I find just the opposite; my bitches tend to be far more independent. Of course, the other thing in a dog's favour is that you do not have to cope with seasons. A bitch comes into season roughly every six months, and this will happen throughout her life, unless you have her spayed, which is an added expense to consider.

Some new owners fear that a male will develop a wanderlust, but, in fact, Labradors are not usually great wanderers. However, as a responsible owner you must ensure your dog – male or female – is not allowed to stray away from your home. The adult male is a little larger and heavier than the female, but he can be just as sweet-tempered, loving and faithful as any bitch. I must admit that I prefer males to females, but I love all my dogs and I realise how much I owe my bitches when they have a litter for me. But I like that extra bit of personality that seems to exude from males – that extra bit of verve and cheekiness, and I feel they do give you that extra bit of love and understanding. However, this is purely a matter of personal choice, and everyone has their own feelings on the subject.

COLOUR

The colour of Labrador you choose is, again, a matter of personal preference. Labradors can be black, yellow or chocolate coloured, and the yellow can range from light cream to red-fox. Regardless of colour, they are all one breed, with the same height, weight, coat texture, temperament and intelligence. There is no escape when it comes to shedding; all three varieties shed their coats, so it is a matter of deciding which colour hairs show up on your carpets! We keep both black and yellow, as I prefer blacks, and my husband has always preferred yellows.

If you are planning to breed, I would not recommend starting with a chocolate, unless you can call on specialised advice from your puppy's breeder. The coat and pigment (skin colour) are not the easiest to keep true unless you know what you are doing. You also have to hope that the sun does not shine all the time, as it is liable to play havoc with the coat colouring. If you want to use your Labrador as a gundog, your local terrain can also play an important part in your choice of colour. If you are surrounded by cornfields, a black dog can really stand out in the stubble, whereas a yellow blends in beautifully. Likewise on moorland, a black blends in better than a pale yellow.

I have found that if you lose a much-loved Labrador, either through old age or any other reason, it is sometimes easier to replace that dog with a puppy of the opposite sex, or with a different coloured pup. Somehow, this stops you from trying to look for the old friend in the new arrival. However, I would stress that every dog has its own personality, so a new dog really is a new dog, regardless of sex or colour. Be it black, yellow or chocolate, dog or bitch, be it an only dog or one of a crowd, if it is a Labrador, you are certain to enjoy it!

FINDING A BREEDER

When you have decided whether you want a puppy or an older animal, a dog or a bitch, and which colour you prefer, the next step is to find a breeder. Always buy from a recognised breeder. The national Kennel Club will help you either by giving you a list of breeders in your area, or by giving you the name and telephone number of the secretary of the nearest local breed club to cover your area. A breed club secretary will probably know which breeders are more likely to suit your requirements, and may even know which breeders have litters due. However, do not be in too much of a hurry. The right puppy from the right breeder will come along in time, and it is worth waiting a little longer to get exactly what you want.

ASSESSING THE PUPPIES

If possible, it is nice to see both the sire and dam of the puppy you are considering, but, as most breeders travel to a stud dog, you will usually only find the dam at the breeder's home or kennel. The breeder will always tell you where the sire is situated, and most breeders are only too happy for you to go and take a look at their stud dogs. When you go to look at a litter, the puppies should be housed in a clean, draught-proof area with enough room to move in, and the pups should look as if they are enjoying life. The accommodation does not need to be very grand – the puppies can be kept in a small room in a house, in part of a barn or an out-building, or in a well-equipped breeding kennel. Cleanliness, light and space show that the breeder knows what he or she is doing.

The puppies themselves should smell 'puppyish'. It is a smell that is hard to describe, but it is clean and wholesome, and it belongs to a puppy that you want to pick up and cuddle. The puppies should be clean and appear healthy, with bright eyes and wagging tails. It is nice to see the puppies come running up to you, but do not completely dismiss the pup that holds its ground and sits and looks at you – this could be the 'thinker' of the litter – the one who is going to weigh everything up. The pup to avoid, unless you are prepared to spend extra time and effort working on it, is the one that runs away looking frightened, and tries to hide. A Labrador Retriever should have a sound, out-going character, and while a more reserved dog could be suitable for an older couple with no children, it is not the one for a noisy family.

There is little point in looking at a litter prior to five weeks of age. The puppies

Your puppy will have to adapt to a whole new way of life when he first arrives in your home.

New experiences will include making friends with all members of the family!

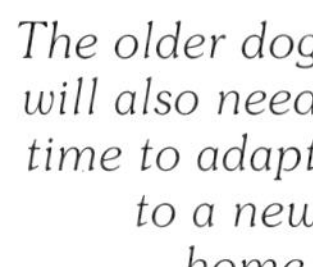

The older dog will also need time to adapt to a new home.

need to be up on their feet and running around, and by this time they will have developed a little bit of personality. When you have picked out your puppy, go back as many times as is convenient for both you and the breeder to see your pup. If, for any reason, you cannot go back too often, do not worry that you might be given the wrong one. All breeders have their own method of marking a pup that is sold. The breeder will give you a date to go and pick up your little treasure, and that is usually at about eight weeks old.

COLLECTING YOUR LABRADOR

Before you go to collect your puppy, you will need to purchase a few items of equipment. As far as food is concerned, be guided by your puppy's breeder, who will usually give you a diet sheet that takes you through the first six months of life. Some breeders provide some food to take the puppy through the first couple of days, otherwise make sure you know what the breeder has been feeding so that you can buy some ready for the new arrival.

You may want to change the diet at a later date, but it is important that you stick to the food your puppy is used to for the first few weeks at least, and then gradually change over, introducing the new food a little at a time. The pup is facing a complete change in his environment, and if you change his feeding habits as well, you could put him through a lot of needless stress. Enquire about the worming programme the breeder has been following, so you can find out when the next treatment is due. You will also need to find out if the puppy has received any inoculations. The breeder should also provide you with a copy of your puppy's pedigree and the paperwork you will need in order to register your puppy with your national Kennel Club.

Try to make the transition period as troublefree as possible for your puppy. Your home represents a whole new way of life. A puppy is leaving his mother and littermates, and has to cope with a whole series of new experiences. If you are buying an older dog, he may have lived in a kennel all his life, and will feel unsure of his new surroundings. In both situations, the dog has to become confident with you and learn your habits. He also has to adjust in many other ways: the time you get up in the morning, the time you go to bed, the time he is fed, and he may have to get used to being exercised on a lead.

If you acquire an older dog, do call him by the name he is used to. If you want to change the name for some reason, do it gradually, but wait until the dog has got used to you and your ways. Do not be jealous if you meet up with the former owners and your dog makes a big fuss of them. After all, the previous owner probably loved him as much as you do now. It is always difficult to re-house a dog when you do not know what the previous owner and home were like, but if you give the dog understanding and let him gain his confidence with you, it will work out. You will both learn from one another – puppy or older dog, it is the start of a new life for both of you.

Chapter Three

CARING FOR YOUR LABRADOR

FEEDING

Now that you have collected your puppy, which is, hopefully, a lively, well-fed little bundle, you will want to know how to keep it that way. If you have bought from a responsible breeder, you will have been supplied with a diet sheet. This will guide you for the first few months.

Do not worry if your puppy goes off his food for the first two or three days. Remember, this is probably the first time that the puppy has been on his own, and he does not have the stimulation of competing for food with his brothers and sisters. Do not despair. If your puppy does not eat his food within ten minutes, just pick up the bowl and wait until the next mealtime.

A puppy will not deliberately starve himself, and if he is more hungry when you offer the next meal, he is more likely to forget his nerves and settle down to his food! It may be advisable to reduce the amount you offer at each mealtime until the pup finds his feet and eats all he is given at the correct time. Remember, if you are serving food from the refrigerator, take it out a little while before you feed, so that it can reach room temperature.

It is advisable to try to keep the puppy on the same feed that the breeder has been using. A change of lifestyle and surroundings are enough for a pup to cope with without having to deal with a new type of food. However, any problems with feeding are likely to be short-lived, as Labradors as a breed are very good 'doers' and they very seldom need to be coaxed to eat – often quite the reverse is true!

Methods of rearing puppies and young stock vary from breeder to breeder. We have all tried the new ways; some have been converted, and some still prefer the old ways. I must admit that I have become a convert, and after the first one to two weeks of giving the puppies their first solid feeds, I go on to feeding one of the 'all-in-one' complete diets. However, I still feed two milk feeds, and I also occasionally add an egg or some cheese. This works for me, and my pups seem to be quite happy and healthy. The new owners also seem to find that the puppies thrive on this diet. Obviously the method you choose is a matter of personal choice, and below is listed the 'traditional' diet, and the 'modern' diet, both of which are suitable for a puppy at eight weeks of age. However, please do as your breeder recommends for the first week or two, and then, if you decide that you want to change, do it slowly, gradually introducing your puppy to the new type of food.

TRADITIONAL

Breakfast (8.00 a.m.): Porridge made with warm milk and baby cereal, or warm milk

Labrador Retrievers are good 'doers', and it is rare to have a fussy feeder.

If you are feeding a complete diet, fresh water must be available at all times.

A dog bed is an important item of equipment, but you would be advised to delay buying one until your puppy has got beyond the chewing stage.

Outside kennels and runs must always be kept scrupulously clean.

with brown bread (a fruit-bowl full). A raw egg can be mixed with this about twice a week. Vitamin supplements can be mixed with this feed.
Lunch (12 noon): 6-8oz raw chopped beef, plus 2-3oz soaked puppy meal. This must be a good-quality wholemeal biscuit.
Snack (3.00 p.m.): Same amount as for breakfast, but use milk and baby rusk, or make a baked egg custard, or half a can of rice pudding.
Supper (6.00 p.m.): Same as for lunch.
Last thing at night: Small biscuit to go to bed with.

Looking at this diet sheet, I wonder when I ever found time to do anything else when I had a litter of puppies to rear. This is one of the reasons that I changed to the following:

MODERN
Breakfast (8.00 a.m.): 4-6oz pre-soaked 'all-in-one feed', or as recommended on the bag of feed. Make sure you choose a good-quality brand of complete diet – be guided by your pup's breeder.
Lunch (12 noon): Powdered goat's milk, or fresh goat's milk, or semi-skimmed cow's milk heated and added to porridge. Feed a fruit-bowl full, using a quarter to a half pint of milk.
Tea (4.00 p.m.): Same as for breakfast.
Supper (6.00 to 7.00 p.m.): Same as lunch. Do not feed this after 7.00 p.m. as it could hinder your house training.
Last thing at night: Small biscuit to go to bed with.

When feeding a complete feed it is important to leave fresh water available at all times. The only drawback is that Labrador puppies like to try to swim in their water bowls! I suggest, therefore, that you remove the water bowl while you are away from the pup for any length of time, such as during the night.

As your puppy grows older, you should start reducing the number of feeds, and increasing the quantity. The first to go are the milk feeds, and I recommend that, at twelve weeks, you cut out the afternoon snack if you are feeding the traditional diet (the 6.00 p.m. feed on the modern diet), and give a little more at the two meat and biscuit or 'all-in-one' feeds. Depending on how your puppy is maturing, cut out the other milk feed at six to eight months, and give just two feeds of meat and meal or two feeds of all-in-one per day. At nine months your young dog will only need one meal a day, and a biscuit to go to bed with. In terms of quantity, this should be 1.5lbs of all-in-one, or 1lb of meat and 8-12oz of biscuit meal a day.

The time of day you choose to feed your dog should be the time that is going to work out the most convenient for you. If you decide on first thing in the morning, then start to take away from the afternoon feed and add to the morning feed, and likewise, in reverse, if you decide to feed in the evening. You will find that milk and eggs are a very controversial feeding subject with veterinarians, but I believe in giving young dogs milk, eggs and milk products. Not only does it gives puppies a change, but I also feel that these products do not harm babies and young children, so they will not harm young puppies. It is certainly true that if you feed a youngster well, you will reap the benefit as the dog matures.

WORMING

When you collect your puppy from the breeder, you should be given details of the worming programme that has been followed, and you will need to know when the next treatment is due. At this age, pups suffer mainly from roundworms, and they are easily treated. Some breeders start to worm at four weeks of age, and then again at two-weekly intervals. Other breeders worm at five and seven weeks, or six to eight weeks.

It is advisable to give your puppy a chance to settle down in his new home and learn to cope with his new feeding schedule etc. before you worm again, and twelve weeks is an ideal time. If your vet sees your pup prior to this age, you can seek advice on a worming routine and you can use the medication your vet recommends. There are also many good patent remedies which are available from pet stores. All are very easy to administer, and it is very rare for a puppy to suffer from any side effects following medication.

It is important to weigh your pup before worming, and then give the dose as directed. Most modern remedies dissolve the worms before they are expelled, but you always check the stools for the twenty-four hour period after worming, and if worms are passed, pick up immediately and burn or dispose of them safely. Make sure you wash your hands afterwards.

Worming is essential to your puppy's welfare. A puppy that is infested with worms cannot get the full benefit from his food, and may develop a nasty, dry cough, bad breath, and dull, dry coat. After you have wormed at twelve weeks, worming should be repeated every six months throughout your dog's life.

INOCULATIONS

Most veterinarians recommend that puppies start their inoculations at twelve weeks of age, but there are a few who like to start them earlier. This may depend on the incidence of diseases in a particular locality, so telephone your vet to find out the local policy, and you can also make an appointment for the first inoculation. Prior to this, make sure that you keep your pup away from places frequented by other dogs. In fact, your puppy should not leave the safety of your garden or yard until after the inoculation programme has been completed.

When you go for the first inoculation, carry your pup and do not put him down in the surgery. The main diseases that are covered are distemper, leptospirosis, hepatitis and parvovirus. Usually, one injection is given and the second is given two weeks later. This will protect your puppy for twelve months. From then onwards, your dog must have an annual booster. Some vets will recommend that you have your dog inoculated against kennel cough, at a later stage. This is well worth doing, not only if you intend to send your dog to a boarding kennel at any time, but also because this disease is very contagious and it can be picked up just by mixing with other dogs in the park or at a dog show.

Remember to keep the inoculation card, which will be issued by your vet, in a safe place. This will give all the dates and details of inoculation, and all reputable boarding kennels will only take dogs with a current inoculation record.

HOUSING

A dog bed is an important item of equipment, but there are a number of points to consider before you rush into an expensive purchase. First of all, there are those

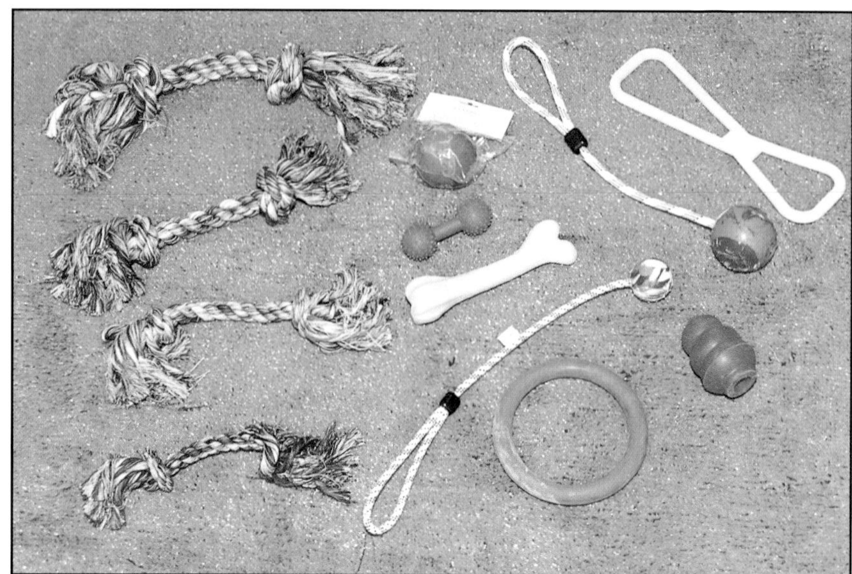

ABOVE: Your puppy will need toys to help him through the teething stage. Make sure you choose tough toys which will stand up to chewing!

BELOW: He will also need feeding and drinking bowls. The stainless steel type are durable and easy to clean.

Do not allow your dog to get possessive over his food. This could lead to aggressive behaviour.

Some owners find a harness useful when teaching a dog to walk to heel

puppy teeth. They might be small, but they are very sharp. You will be surprised how quickly wicker unravels when chewed by those little needles, and you will be surprised how much wicker there is in a basket when it has all unravelled!

A large cardboard box is a good choice for your pup's first bed. Make sure there are no metal pins in it, and you can cut the front down so that the pup can get in and out easily. Alternatively, you could buy a rigid plastic bed. They are not too expensive, and so it is best to buy a medium-sized one with a view to buying a larger one when the dog is fully grown. These are harder to chew than a wicker basket, and they are also easier to clean.

Most puppies are naturally clean in their bed, so you can put a blanket or towel in the bottom for comfort. Some pups will not be so obliging, in which case a good layer of newspapers in the bottom will have to suffice for a while. Your yellow puppy may look a little grubby, as the print often rubs off from the newspapers, but it will not do any harm. If you want to avoid this, you can use shredded paper for bedding. However, you would be advised to wait a while before you give your puppy a pet duvet. If your puppy chews an old blanket, it is not so hard on the pocket; it is easier to clear up the mess, and it is not so harmful if any pieces are swallowed. I find that fleecy, polyester bedding strips are ideal. They are warm and comfortable for the dog; they can be machine-washed, and they are difficult to chew.

You must also decide where your puppy is going to sleep, and this is obviously a matter of personal choice. However, you must ensure that the bed is located somewhere that is free of draughts and out of the main thoroughfare, so that the dog can have a good rest in warmth and comfort. If you choose a room that has a washable floor with no carpets, such as the kitchen or utility room, it will make life easier. You must be prepared for a few 'mistakes' to start with, and a mop and bucket is so much easier to use than a shampoo machine!

Make sure that there are no electric wires near the pup's bed, as this is just the sort of thing a puppy likes to try his teeth out on – and the results could be disastrous. Hopefully, your puppy will be less likely to chew after cutting the second teeth, which usually happens from around twelve to fifteen weeks. When your dog is adult, you can buy whatever type of bed you desire – with a best duvet or blanket in the bottom – and, of course, you can put it in the sitting room on your best carpet, or even beside your bed. Be warned though, your Labrador may start off in the basket, but at some time in the early hours the temptation to climb on to your bed may become too much, and an 80lb Labrador makes a poor bed fellow!

OUTSIDE KENNELS

If you are going to kennel your dog outside, the same basic formula applies. However, instead of a cardboard box, use a wooden box and, if you do not have a heat-lamp, a box with a lid on helps to keep a puppy warm. This is not so important if you are kennelling two dogs together, as they have each other for warmth, but if the kennel is five or six feet high there is an awful lot of space to be heated, so a lid approximately three feet above the bed makes for a smaller area.

Make sure the bed is off the ground and that the pup can get in and out of it easily. Wood shavings make an excellent form of bedding; you will need a board three-quarters of the way along the front of the bed and some six inches high to keep them in. Shredded paper or the fleecy polyester beddings are also good for outdoor use. I do not advocate either hay or straw as bedding. They both seem to harbour too many parasites for my liking.

Leave an area in front of the bed, which is covered with newspapers or sawdust to mop up accidents. This can be easily picked up and replaced in the morning. Remember, the first few nights that a puppy is left on his own can be a bit noisy – so be firm!

GROOMING

The Labrador is a short-coated breed, and so it does not require a great deal of grooming. All you will need are the basic tools, such as a good brush and a comb, and a weekly grooming session will be sufficient to keep your dog in good condition. If your dog rolls in something horrible, or is losing his coat, a bath with a good-quality medicated shampoo will help get rid of dirt and also the loose hairs. A rub-down with a towel, and then a brush and comb, and your dog is as good as new.

At the weekly grooming session, check your dog's ears. If the ears are dirty, buy some ear cleaner and use as directed, removing any dirt from the outer part of the ear with cotton wool. Do not use cotton buds or probe too deeply into the ear. Your dog's nails should be kept short. Regular road-walking should keep them in trim, but if they grow too long, you will need to snip off the points with a pair of nail-clippers.

A spray with a good flea control every two weeks will keep your dog free from fleas. A healthy dog will have a good glossy coat, but most Labradors love to be brushed. This also helps to bring the new coat back in a little faster when your dog is shedding.

The Labrador has an inborn instinct to retrieve, and most dogs will enjoy learning the exercise.

Chapter Four

TRAINING YOUR LABRADOR

Everyone wants to own a well-behaved, obedient dog that they can take anywhere and which will not be a nuisance to anyone. Like all things that are worth achieving, this takes some hard work, but as a responsible dog owner you should be prepared to take on the commitment of training your Labrador to become a well-mannered, sociable individual.

HOUSE TRAINING

This is the first important lesson that you will want to teach your puppy. Being a highly intelligent breed, Labrador Retrievers are usually quick to catch on, once they know what is expected. In all training, it is important to be consistent, and this is particularly the case with house training.

The correct way to put on a choke chain: If the chain runs through the top of the ring, it will release automatically.

As soon as you have fed your pup, take him out to the same area and give a command such as "Be quick" or "Be clean", making sure you always use the same command. As soon as your puppy does what is required, give plenty of praise. You must be prepared to wait until you get the desired result – the puppy will not learn anything if you just let him out in the garden on his own. Inevitably, there will be times when you wait for what seems like an eternity, and when you give up, the puppy goes straight into the house and then performs. In this instance, scold your puppy, and take him outside again. Never ignore the mistakes.

Do not leave it too long between visits outside. You will be surprised how often a pup needs to go. But the basic rule is to take the puppy out immediately after feeding, and every time he wakes up from a rest.

PUPPY TRAINING

Puppies are like children, and both should be properly brought up so that they are well-behaved and a pleasure to have around. The golden rule is to start as you mean to go on. When you say "No", you must mean it. A puppy must understand what is required, and so you must praise your puppy when he is good, and scold him when he is naughty.

A puppy has a lot to learn in the first few months of his life. He has to adapt to his new family, his new home, as well as to many new experiences outside the home. This vital period of socialisation is the key to having a well-behaved, well-adapted dog. If you give your puppy time at this stage, you will find it pays dividends when you get down to more serious training. Although you cannot venture far afield until your puppy has completed his inoculation programme, you can still make progress. The first step is build up a bond with your puppy. If your puppy learns to trust you, he will be reassured by your presence when he is confronted by strange things, which he might find alarming.

The first time you go out with your puppy, talk reassuringly to him all the time. This keeps your puppy's attention on you, and you will be able to coax him along when he confronts the hustle and bustle of a busy street and the noise of traffic. If your puppy is frightened, do not force him to confront whatever is frightening him. Give your puppy a chance to watch what is going on while you give lots of praise and reassurance, and you will find that, in most cases, your puppy's natural curiosity will win the day!

LEAD TRAINING

If you have bought a puppy with the intention of showing it, never leave a collar on all the time, as it makes the hair around the neck flatter, and this does not help the dog to present a clean outline in the ring. However, a collar is a must for a pet dog. The first step is to get your puppy used to the feel of a collar. It is a good idea to start off with a soft collar, but do not buy anything expensive – you will find that it will not be long before your puppy grows out of it.

As soon as your puppy accepts the collar, you can attach the lead. To begin with, just allow your puppy to walk around the living room, and follow where the puppy chooses to go. If all goes well, you can proceed to walk up and down the garden path, encouraging your puppy to follow you. It is a good idea to have a biscuit or ball in your hand, and if the pup protests or puts the brakes on, entice him to walk towards you. Play with him with the lead on and, as he grows older, make him walk beside you, usually on your left-hand side. When he pulls, pull him back and give the command "Heel".

If you use a choke collar, never leave it on the pup when he is alone, as this could be fatal if it gets caught on anything. When using the choke, remember to release your hold on it when the pup stops pulling. If you start your lead training at about ten weeks, your puppy should be ready to walk on the road as soon as the inoculation programme is completed.

Do not allow children to take a puppy out alone on the road. A quick pull from a puppy can catch a child unawares, and this could end in disaster for the puppy, the child, or both.

BASIC COMMANDS

Do not make the mistake of thinking that you cannot train your puppy until he is six months old. A puppy as young as eight weeks old is very receptive, and there is no reason why you should not introduce basic commands, building up to basic Obedience exercises. However, it is important to remember that your puppy is still very young, and his concentration span will be very limited. Keep your 'lessons' very short, give plenty of praise, and always end on a good note. If your puppy is enjoying himself, he is far more likely to respond to your wishes. If you feel tired or short-tempered, do not attempt to train your puppy on that day.

Lessons should be fun – you will achieve nothing if you find yourself getting cross or frustrated. If your puppy fails to understand what is required, go back to an exercise you know he can do. In this way, you will end your training session positively, rather than with a sense of failure. The next time you train your puppy go back to the 'difficult' exercise, and you will almost certainly make progress.

THE "SIT"

This is an easy command to teach, and it will be useful throughout your dog's life. A good time to teach your puppy to sit is at mealtimes. As you offer your puppy his meal, give the command "Sit", place your hand on your puppy's hindquarters and exert slight pressure. In no time, your puppy will sit every time a meal is offered, and will also have learnt the command "Sit", which you can then use in other situations.

THE "DOWN"

This is a straightforward exercise, but it could be a life-saver if your dog learns to respond instantly to the command "Down", no matter what the situation is. Tone of voice is important when giving this command; it is important to use a deep, firm voice as this aids the puppy's understanding. Start with your puppy in the "Sit", and give the command "Down", applying slight pressure to the dog's shoulders and giving a downward tug with the lead. Hold your dog in the "Down" for a few seconds, giving plenty of praise, before releasing him.

THE "STAY"

This exercise should be built up gradually – there is no point in being ambitious before your puppy understands what is required – you will just end up with a thoroughly confused dog. To start with, keep your puppy on a lead, and give the command "Sit". Then, back away from your puppy, just to the end of the lead, and give the command "Stay", using the appropriate hand signal – hand held upwards,

The "Sit" can be taught by applying light pressure to the dog's hindquarters and giving the command "Sit".

Teaching the "Down"

Start with your dog in the "Sit", give the command "Down", applying pressure to the shoulders and tugging the lead downwards.

Bend down with your dog, helping him to understand what is required.

Keep your dog in the "Down" for a few seconds, and then release him, giving plenty of praise.

palm facing towards the puppy. When the exercise is finished, return to your puppy's side and give plenty of praise. When you are confident that your puppy understands what is required, you can gradually increase the distance from the puppy using a check cord, and eventually, you can leave your puppy without a lead.

THE RECALL

Your puppy will learn the command "Come" in the first few days. Just call your puppy by his name, and add the command – "Rover, Come". Encourage your puppy to come to you by crouching down to his level with your arms out-stretched. This exercise can be developed as the puppy grows older, in conjunction with the "Stay", until you complete a proper recall. However, do not be tempted to rush basic training.

Start with your puppy on the lead or check cord on your left-hand side and give the command "Sit".Then, give the command "Wait", and back away from your puppy, giving the hand signal to stay with palm facing your dog. Eventually you will be able to turn and walk away from your puppy, but this should only be introduced when you are confident that your puppy will stay in position. When you are ready, stop, repeat the command "Wait", reinforcing this with the appropriate hand signal. Wait a couple of seconds and call your puppy in – "Rover, Come" opening out your arms to welcome your puppy, and reward with lots of praise. Do not confuse your puppy by calling him to you when you have given the command "Stay". The "Stay" exercise and the recall should be separated in your dog's mind, and so it is easier to use a different command i.e. "Wait" when you are doing a recall.

TRAINING TARGETS

By the time your Labrador is six months old, you hopefully have a reasonably well-mannered dog, who is pretty reliable. Your puppy is house trained, lead trained, and comes when he is called. He may even sit and stay on command. You will have discovered by this time that the only way to teach your dog anything is by repetition. Repeat a lesson over and over again until your pup has absorbed it, and do not go on to the next lesson until you are satisfied this is so. Have patience (loads of it!), and be very liberal with your praise. Above all, the training sessions must be fun for the pup. If you get bogged down, and tempers get frayed, training takes twice as long, and you are unlikely to achieve such good results.

The Labrador Retriever is one of the Gundog or Sporting breeds, and the basic instincts to retrieve, and to please, are there in your puppy, waiting for you to further the education. This is an intelligent breed, and your Labrador is likely to become bored if he is left completely to his own devices. The type of training you give your dog depends on what you want to achieve. You may be content with a well-behaved family companion, or you may be more competitive and want to have a go at Obedience or Agility competitions. Equally, you may have bought your puppy to be a shooting companion, or you may want to compete in Working Tests and have dreams of running in Field Trials. Whatever area you decide to get involved with, make sure you go to a good training club run by people who are well qualified in their field. There are also many excellent books on Gundog and Obedience training, and these are written by experts with a proven track record on their subject. In the scope of this book, I will merely outline the essentials of what is required, and hope that you go on to pursue your new hobby in more depth.

OBEDIENCE TRAINING

All dogs should be taught basic Obedience, and many owners are quite happy when their dog masters the basics. However, some owners are more competitive, and the dogs certainly seem to enjoy the stimulation of responding to increasingly complex commands. The Labrador is certainly intelligent enough, and there is no reason why your dog cannot do well in this field. It is important to start when your pup is about six months of age, and you cannot expect to join in more advanced Obedience classes until your dog is walking on a lead, sitting, or perhaps sitting and staying, and coming when called.

Many training clubs run puppy classes, and these will help you to teach your pup the basics. This is done in the company of other pups, and so it is an excellent way of teaching your dog to concentrate despite distractions. These classes are usually run weekly, some two-weekly, depending on availability of venue or trainer, and they will expect you to continue training on your own at home. As with retrieving classes, the trainer is always someone who is qualified in this branch of dog training and has the ability to teach others. Nine times out of ten, it is the owner who needs the training, and Obedience trainers do seem to have the knack of training both dog and owner.

One word of advice – if you intend to show your dog, mention this to the trainer, and the "Stand" will probably be substituted for "Sit" when you come to a halt. This is because the "Sit" would be a positive disadvantage in the show ring, when the aim is to get your dog to pose in order to show himself off to full advantage. Some dog shows have Obedience trials at the show, and the dogs entered in these need not be entered for the show. There is a set programme for each test, and a judge calculates the points to be awarded. There are also shows for Obedience dogs only.

If you get really hooked on competitive Obedience there are plenty of titles to be won. In the UK these include Companion Dog (CD), Utility Dog (UD), and Tracking Dog (TD), in ascending order of difficulty. In North America the corresponding titles are: Companion Dog (CD), Companion Dog Excellent (CDX), Utility Dog (UD), Tracking Dog (TD), and Tracking Dog Excellent (TDX).

AGILITY TRAINING

Agility is an increasingly popular activity, and both owners and dogs get a lot of fun from it. Obviously, the Labrador is not as fast as some breeds such as the Border Collie, but accuracy is also important, and the Labrador will have no trouble in negotiating the obstacles.

The apparatus for agility competitions includes an 'A' frame, a dog walk, a see-saw, hurdles, a tunnel, a tyre and weaving poles. It is essential that you do not attempt to train your Labrador for agility until he is at least twelve months of age. The exertion involved in this sport could prove hazardous to a growing puppy.

However, while you are waiting to enroll at an agility training club, the time can be usefully spent working on basic Obedience. Your dog will be working off-lead, and therefore you must have complete control over him. The obstacles must be tackled when you give the command, and the dog must not leap off before he has negotiated the obstacle correctly. Instant response to the commands of "Wait" and "Down" are essential.

It is also important to have built up a good relationship with your Labrador, as you are asking him to attempt tasks that are well outside his normal compass. However,

Teaching the Recall

Give your dog the command "Wait", and give the appropriate hand signal.

Walk to the end of the check cord and turn round and face your dog. Give the command "Come".

When your dog returns to you, give plenty of praise.

Teaching the Retrieve

Your dog must learn to sit at your side while you throw the dummy.

Most Labradors are natural retrievers, and will run out to fetch the dummy when the command "Fetch" is given.

A fully-trained Labrador Retriever at work, bringing game safely and tenderly back to the handler.

once the dogs are familiar with the obstacles, they thoroughly enjoy the challenge of tackling them – and in most cases, the hardest job is to slow the dog down in order that he listens to instructions. Many newcomers think their dog will be frightened by the tunnel, but for some reason, nearly all dogs love running through this piece of apparatus. The weaving poles pose the greatest challenge, particularly for the bigger dogs. With this exercise, there is no substitute for practise.

The agility course is tackled against the clock, and time is lost for faults on the way round. Both dogs and handlers have to be fit to be successful in this activity. However, even if you do not reach the highest level of competition, this is a marvellous way of channeling your dog's energies, and building up a good working relationship.

GUN TRAINING

GETTING STARTED

If you decide that you want to gun-train your puppy, it is a good idea to join your local Labrador club, or a local gundog club. These clubs run gundog training days, usually supervised by someone who has great knowledge and understanding of both dogs and novice handlers. Training in this atmosphere enables your dog to get accustomed to working in the company of other dogs and to the various distractions he might not otherwise encounter if he was trained on his own.

Most clubs of this sort have access to land of varying types, plough, scrubland, woods and water – you do not have to own a country estate to train your gundog! I know of quite a few people who, when they started gun-training, lived in town with a postage-stamp sized garden, a park nearby, and just the monthly visit to the training classes, and they have become well-known and successful in the Field Trial world.

When you attend your first training session, you will soon realise that there are a few items that you will have to buy. Firstly the 'dummy' or dummies, as you will need several. The dummy looks like a filled sock, usually made of green canvas, and filled with sand. There is a rope loop on one end to enable it to be thrown. Another dummy will be filled with a floatable material for use in water retrieves. They may be on sale at the classes, or you may have to find a local gun-shop. Of course, if you are terribly clever with your hands, you could make your own! You will need a whistle, this is an absolute must for gundog training, and the sort you need will be of the stag-horn type. Do not go for the referee's whistle (the sort with a pea in it) or the old type police whistle. The stag-horn has just the right pitch for retrieving work, and all the old hands use them.

Dogs must be taught to stop on the whistle, and also to come (quickly!) on the same whistle. In the novice class, all the other dogs and owners will be just like yourself, so there is no need to worry that you are going to make complete fools of yourselves. There is always a great deal of good-natured rivalry and leg-pulling at these sorts of gatherings. When you watch the advanced dogs doing all sorts of clever things with double dummies and unseen retrieves, just remember – they also started in the novice class.

BASIC EXERCISES

You will find that some dogs are naturally better than others, and, unfortunately, there is also the minority that just do not want to know. It is the same with the owners: some have infinite patience and the knack of bringing out the best in their dogs, others just do not seem to communicate with their dogs at all, and they lack the patience and understanding that is required to make a good handler. You cannot advance in your training until your pup is 'steady'. In other words, your Labrador must "Sit", "Stay" and "Come" to command every time. The dog must understand that this is his 'work', and all thoughts of play must disappear.

You will require a long length of cord to be used as a check-cord. This is really just an extra long lead. A washing line is ideal; it is light, and it is not so thin that it will cut your hand if the pup makes a sudden lunge. Sit your pup at heel, *always* on your left side. In fact, all training is carried out with your dog on your left side, for the simple reason that this leaves your right side free to use your shot-gun. With the pup at heel, you will then walk a few paces forward, first with the pup on the check-cord, keeping him nicely to heel. This exercise will probably be in company with other dogs and handlers, so there will be many distractions at first.

Having accomplished this exercise a few times successfully, your instructor will then take you on to stage two – walking in line with the dog off the check-cord and at heel. Confusion may reign for a while but, by this stage, you should at least have some measure of control over your dog. Spend as much time as you can spare on this exercise, both on your own at home and in company. Steadiness under all conditions is most important if you are going to graduate to the next stage, the retrieve.

RETRIEVING

We always started our pups retrieving at home, just to ensure that they do retrieve. There is nothing more embarrassing than standing in line for your first retrieve, watching the dummy land in full view and not too far away, giving the command to your pup, and then wishing the ground would open up and swallow you as he yawns, scratches and rolls over on his back! A long passage-way is an ideal place for training pups. The dog runs straight out and straight back with the dummy – there is nowhere else to go. Make sure you have lots of tidbits, and always give plenty of praise when the dog returns with the dummy. This simple procedure certainly beats chasing your puppy over a forty-acre field in order to get the dummy back!

At the training class, your pup should now be walking at heel on and off the lead. At this stage, the line of handlers and their dogs move off, and at a command, they stop. A dummy will be thrown for you, and, when you are instructed, you will send the pup in to retrieve it. Generally, on the first retrieve, the check-cord is used, just to remove the temptation of the pup parading up and down the line of dogs with the dummy in his mouth. If your dog comes straight back to you, make him sit, still holding the dummy, and gently take it from the pup. Then give plenty of praise.

Naturally, this exercise will be repeated many times until the check-cord can be dispensed with, and the pup is going further out for his retrieves. You will gradually proceed from here until your dog is retrieving 'unseen' dummies, doing double dummies, retrieving from water, obeying hand-signals, getting used to gun-fire, and, eventually, picking up cold game (birds shot at an earlier date and kept frozen until needed). Introduction to gunfire should be a gradual process. Most people start by making a sudden noise while the puppy is feeding and is, therefore, distracted. This can be built up until the sound of gunfire leaves your dog totally unperturbed.

The Labrador Retriever is ideally suited to working as a guide dog, with its intelligent approach to life, and its friendly, confident disposition.

The fully-trained guide dog has a special relationship with his blind owner.

At last, the magic day arrives when your fully-trained dog retrieves the real thing to hand. There is no lovelier sight than seeing the dog that you have trained returning with the game you sent him to retrieve. It is just you and your dog at that moment. You both have implicit trust in one another, and the expression in the dog's eyes as he comes to hand is what can only be described as the typical Labrador expression.

A well-trained dog is welcome on any shoot, and even if you are not fortunate enough to belong to a shoot, you will always be in demand for 'picking-up' – you might even get paid! A pair of good waterproof boots, and thornproof, windproof and waterproof clothing, in country shades, are essential.

FIELD TRIALS

Competing in Field Trials is another thing entirely from keeping and training a shooting companion. In fact, I believe that field trialling has become so specialised that you really should purchase your puppy from a kennel that has a reputation for producing Field Trial dogs. Take advice from Field Trial trainers. This is one step further than the odd days picking up or your own rough-shoot. Speed, instant response to commands and a highly developed scenting ability are absolute musts in this highly competitive sport. There are a few people who run their show dogs and shooting dogs in trials with some success, but it must be said that the top honours generally go to the dogs specially bred for the purpose.

THE VERSATILE RETRIEVER

Although first and foremost the Labrador Retriever is a gundog, the breed's outstanding temperament, intelligence and trainability have led to other uses being evolved for it over the years.

GUIDE DOGS FOR THE BLIND

Labradors are used as guide dogs for the blind worldwide. In the early days of the charity, German Shepherd Dogs were used, and although they are still employed in this role, Labradors and Labrador-crosses are now used most extensively for guide dog work. There are a number of reasons why the breed suits this work so well. The Labrador is medium sized, and has a low-maintenance coat, which a blind person can care for without undue difficulty. The breed is intelligent, willing to please, and easy to train. Above all, the typical Labrador temperament is sound and steady – a dog that will cope calmly and sensibly in all situations. It is loyal and affectionate, and can withstand the stress of training better than a more sensitive breed.

Many Labrador breeders have provided guide dogs over the years, although now the Guide Dogs for the Blind Association in Britain runs its own breeding programme, which is tailormade to produce the type of dog that is most suitable for guide dog work. The success of the Association's breeding programme is reflected in the pass rate that it achieves in its litters – nearly always over seventy per cent and sometimes up to one hundred per cent. Kennels are of a very high standard, and the kennel staff are given a superb grounding in kennel management and puppy/dog handling.

Puppies are taken into the homes of puppy walkers, and here they learn the basics of obedience and they are exposed to as many different situations as possible. It costs a great deal of money to train each dog to the exacting standard required, so, if it does not come up to scratch as far as temperament and reliability is concerned at this early age, there is no point in proceeding any further. One day the dog will be responsible for a blind person's life, so it has to be one hundred per cent trustworthy in all circumstances it may encounter.

Having passed the initial test, which is usually when the puppy is nine to twelve months of age, the trainee guide dog is now ready to go to work. It is returned to one of the training centres where, among other things, it is taught the use of the harness, the correct procedure for crossing the road, avoiding obstacles and generally guiding its owner in a busy urban environment. Some centres do allow visitors and it is well worth a visit to watch the dogs in training.

The final step is matching the dog to a blind person and then dog and owner undergo a period of residential training. After qualifying at the training centre, specialised staff provide aftercare with a series of home visits to ensure that the new partnership is working well. A guide dog works hard and, although in most cases it has a very enjoyable off-duty life, the age span for a working guide dog is usually only about eight or nine years. These dogs are then usually rehoused with either friends or relatives of the blind owner

HEARING DOGS FOR THE DEAF

This is a relatively new role for dogs and, again, Labradors have adapted well to the work. The dogs are trained to run towards the sound of a noise e.g. when the telephone or doorbell rings, or when the timer on the cooker goes off. This attracts the attention of the deaf person, so that they know what is happening and can then deal with it.

DOGS FOR THE DISABLED

This is a relatively new way of using dogs, and it has been found that trainee guide dogs who failed to make the grade can be used in this capacity, following extra specialised training. These dogs do an invaluable job helping their owners around the house, opening doors, picking up the telephone receiver, switching lights on and off, taking the milk bottles outside, and fetching articles that are required. I have seen one emptying the clothes from a tumble-drier, pulling them out gently with its teeth and putting them into into a laundry basket.

THERAPY DOGS

Therapy dogs, known as PAT dogs in Britain, do a marvellous job visiting hospitals, residential homes for the elderly and schools. Labradors are used extensively for this work, as their friendly outgoing temperament is ideal. Many a child has got over a fear of dogs because a Labrador has visited the school, where it has stood patiently and allowed the children to pat it, or even walk it a short way on the lead. This is an ideal way of teaching children how to behave with a dog.

In a hospital ward, a Labrador seems to be just the right height for a patient to be able to pat its head without too much effort, and this communication has tremendous therapeutic value. In residential homes for the elderly, a visit from a dog is greatly looked forward to, and provides a great talking point for the residents.

POLICE AND SNIFFER DOGS

The German Shepherd Dog is the most commonly used police dog, but Labradors

The Labrador Retriever has an excellent sense of smell and is used by the security forces to sniff out drugs and explosives.

are also used a great deal. They are trained in most aspects of police work, tracking, guarding, latterly as sniffer dogs to sniff out drugs and explosives.

Because of its high degree of intelligence as a breed, a Labrador can be trained to be aggressive on command. This is a reversal of the usual temperament of the breed, but apparently it is a lesson that, once learned, they excel at. The favoured colour for this work is black, although all three colours are used.

Training dogs for use as sniffer dogs for drug and explosives started in the 1960s. Many breeds were tested and, at that time, Labradors topped the poll, although Springer Spaniels are now very popular. The Spaniels are smaller, and as they often have to be lifted up and put through windows or into loft-spaces, you can see why the Springer wins over an eighty-pound Labrador!

Chapter Six

IN THE SHOW RING

THE BREED STANDARD

The Breed Standard is a written description of what the ideal Labrador Retriever should look like. It also takes into account character, temperament, and movement. All Breed Standards were originally drawn up by pioneers of the breed in question, and various changes have taken place over the years. The Labrador's country of origin is Britain, as this is where the breed was developed, despite its early links with Canada. The British Breed Standard is therefore adopted by all countries governed by the Federation Cynologique Internationale, which includes most European countries and Australia. The USA has its own Breed Standard, but this differs very little from the British version. We are lucky in having a breed where the majority of fanciers are united in their perception of what a Labrador should look like.

The Breed Standard is a blueprint to help breeders and judges to know what to look for and what to aim for in their breeding. If there was not a Standard laid down, in years to come the Labrador as we know it today might look entirely different – and this would be a disaster. For even if you have no plans to show your Labrador or to breed from it, you still want your pet to have all the typical Labrador qualities, in terms of both looks and character.

GENERAL APPEARANCE

The Labrador should be a strongly built, very active dog. It should be broad in the skull, broad and deep through the chest and ribs, broad and strong over the loins and hindquarters. The overall impression should be of a strong, muscular dog. The coat is an important feature of the breed. It must be close and short, with a hard feeling to the hand. The undercoat must be very dense (to help keep out the water). You can see the undercoat when you turn back the top coat along the ribs. It is the short, fluffy coat underneath.The coat must have no featherings and it should be free from feather or wave. The top coat must feel fairly hard.

CHARACTER

The character and temperament of the Labrador Retriever is second to none. The British Standard sums this up with its description of an intelligent dog, keen and biddable, with a strong will to please. It has a kindly nature, and is an adaptable and devoted companion.

HEAD

The typical Labrador head is large with a broad skull. It should have a pronounced

Anatomy of the Labrador Retriever

1. Muzzle
2. Stop
3. Occiput
4. Withers
5. Back
6. Croup
7. Tail
8. Hock
9. Stifle
10. Tuck up
11. Chest
12. Pastern

The typical Labrador Retriever head is large with a broad skull, and the eyes should express intelligence and good humour.

stop (the step-up from the muzzle to the skull), so that the skull is not in a straight line with the nose. The head must be clean cut without fleshy cheeks. The jaw should be of a medium length, and the muzzle should be free from any snipiness (not too pointed or weak). The Labrador has an excellent sense of smell, and so it should have a wide nose, and the nostrils should be well developed.

EYES

Expression is all-important, and in a Labrador this seems to come from the eyes. They should be medium in size, expressing intelligence and good temper. A round eye can give a dog a hard expression. The eyes should be brown or hazel.

EARS

These should not be too large or heavy. They should be set rather far back to hang close to the head. A rounded tip to the ear can make a dog look houndy. If the ears are too small and carried high on the head, this can look a little like a terrier. Both of these are judged as faults in the Labrador.

MOUTH

The teeth should be strong and sound and should have a scissor bite i.e. the lower teeth just behind, but touching, the upper teeth. The Labrador is a retriever and is expected to carry pheasants or hares, so it is very important that the jaw is correct, as imperfections could cause damage to whatever they carry, or may cause discomfort to the dog, making it drop its retrieve.

NECK

This should be clean, strong and powerful and set into well-placed shoulders. When seen in outline, there should be no loose flesh under the chin, known as throatiness, and the shoulders should be long and sloping. An upright shoulder makes a dog move incorrectly, giving it a stilted movement instead of a long extended easy gait.

FOREQUARTERS

The fore legs should be well boned and straight from the shoulder to the ground when viewed from either the front, or from the side. The chest should be well developed, but the dog should not look too wide or too narrow in front.

BODY

There must be plenty of heart room, and the body must have well-sprung ribs. The Labrador should be short-coupled i.e. the part of the body between the ribs and the hindquarters should be short in length. It is sometimes better for a bitch to be slightly longer in her couplings, thus enabling her to carry a litter easier.

HINDQUARTERS

The loins should be well developed and not sloping towards the tail. The stifles (the 'knee') should be well turned. The hocks (the 'heel') should be slightly bent and the dog must not stand cow-hocked i.e. the hocks bending in towards each other. When moving, they should not move too close or too wide behind.

FEET
These should be round and compact with well-arched toes and well-developed pads.

TAIL
This is one of the distinctive features of the breed. It should be very thick at the base, gradually tapering to the tip, of medium length, practically free from feathering, and clothed all around with the Labrador's short thick coat, giving a peculiar rounded appearance. This is known as an 'otter' tail, and if you look at an otter's tail you can see why. The tail can be carried gaily, but it must never curl over the back.

MOVEMENT
The Labrador's movement should be free and effortless. From the front the elbows should be held neatly to the body, and from the rear the hindlegs should move as nearly parallel as possible.

COLOUR
There are three colours: Black, Yellow and Chocolate. These must be solid colours, although a small white spot on the chest would not be penalised in the show ring. The yellow can range from cream to fox-red, and the chocolate can range from light sedge to chocolate, according to the American Breed Standard, although the British Standard confines itself to liver/chocolate.

SIZE AND WEIGHT
The desired height for dogs is 22-22.5 inches (56-57cms). In America males are larger with a stipulated height of 22.5-24.5 inches. The British Standard asks for bitches to be 21.5 inches in height (54-56cms), in America the requirement is 21.5-23.5 inches. Weight is not stipulated in the British Breed Standard, but the American Standard states that dogs in working condition should weigh between 60-75 pounds and bitches should be between 55-70 pounds.

SUMMARY
The Breed Standard attempts to paint a picture of the perfect Labrador, and, of course, the 'perfect' dog is unlikely ever to be produced. Therefore, breeders and judges assess dogs in terms of how closely they conform to the Breed Standard. When all is said and done, the aim of everyone who has the breed's interests at heart is to promote a typical, sound dog, that has the unique Labrador character.

THE SHOW RING
Dog shows are, first and foremost, beauty shows, and the best-looking specimen of the breed, in the opinion of the judge, is the one that wins. However, they do have a more serious side to them. A dog show is the breeders' shop window, where only the best dogs should be exhibited, and where breeders can assess their own, and other breeders' stock. A lot can be learned about a strain of Labradors being exhibited at shows.

The other side of showing is the fun – the thrill of winning, be it just a reserve, or even the fact that your dog was given a second look by the judge, or a compliment from someone sitting at the ringside. If you ever achieve a first prize, it is an unforgettable thrill, and the card or rosette can be placed in a prominent place to be

In the UK, Championship Shows are 'benched' and every dog is allocated its own bench. This is not the case in the USA.

The judge must assess each dog, evaluating how closely it conforms to the Breed Standard.

If you get bitten by the show-going bug, you will soon be taking a car-load of Labrador Retrievers to a show!

a talking point for years! However, you must always remember that, in your heart, you took the "best dog ever" to the show, and that you are taking that "best dog ever" home – with or without a prize.

Do not give up after only one show if your dog is unplaced. All judges assess the dogs according to the Kennel Club Breed Standard, but we all differ slightly when it comes to interpreting the written word. Therefore, all judges have their own opinions, and they may rate the same dogs differently – this is one of the fascinations of dog showing. So, if you do not win one day, providing your dog is up to show standard, you might win the next. You will also make a lot of friends at shows, and you will probably get to parts of the country that you would never have dreamed of visiting. I would add one note of warning: once you have been bitten by the show bug, you could find it very difficult to give up!

The way dogs shows are run, and the scoring used for a dog to become a Champion, varies from country to country. Generally speaking, Britain operates under the auspices of the English Kennel Club, the USA is governed by the American Kennel Club, the Canadian Kennel Club oversees Canada, and Europe holds dog shows under the jurisdiction of the Federation Cynologique Internationale (FCI).

I lived in America for nine years, managing a show kennel, and so I had to adapt to the American way of doing things. I feel that different countries can learn a lot from each other, and over the last few years I have seen quite a few American innovations being introduced to Britain. The layout of British shows is improving and tenting is following the American style. One major difference is that professional handlers are used far more frequently in the USA. This is largely because the size of the country would make it impossible for most owners to campaign their dogs. Professional handlers therefore take on a number of dogs and travel from show to show in a mobile home. The standard of handling and presentation is top-class.

There are dog show circuits, such as the Cherry Blossom circuit, held on the East Coast in the Spring, and as many as eight or nine shows may be held in a period of ten to twelve days.

TYPES OF SHOWS

BRITAIN

EXEMPTION: These shows are usually run in aid of charity. They have at least four pedigree dog classes and the rest are 'fun' classes such as 'The dog that looks most like its owner' or 'The dog with the waggiest tail'. These are usually judged either by a very well-known judging personality, the local vet or his wife, or a local judge who is just starting out on a judging career. This is good fun day out, and it is very good grounding for young puppies and handlers.

SANCTION/LIMIT: To exhibit at this type of show you have to be a member of the Canine Society running the show. Good representatives of your breed can be seen at these shows, but Champions cannot be exhibited.

OPEN: This is another step up the ladder, and as the name implies, it is open to all-comers. You will see some top-quality Labradors, and you will see some excellent handling by exhibitors in the ring.

CHAMPIONSHIP: These are the shows where the prized Challenge Certificates are allocated, and you will see the cream of the breed competing for honours. The judge awards a dog CC and a bitch CC, and then Best of Breed is awarded. This dog will go forward to represent the breed in the Gundog Group judging, and the winner of each Group competes for Best in Show. In order to become a Champion in Britain, a dog must win a total of three Challenge Certificates, awarded by three different judges. In order to do this, a dog must beat all-comers, including Champions.

In Britain, Championship shows are 'benched', which means that your dog will be allocated a number and a bench, where he must be must be accommodated during the show (when he is not being exercised or competing in the ring).

AMERICA

MATCHES: The local All Breed and Specialty Clubs will probably hold one or two Matches a year. These are advertised in the canine press, giving details of breeds, classes and judges. Entries are made on the morning of the show. They are often used as a training ground for people who are aspiring to judge at Championship show level. Classes usually range from Puppy through Novice to Open. Champions are not eligible to compete in Matches.

CHAMPIONSHIP SHOWS: These can be All Breed, Group or Breed shows. They are advertised in the canine press, and premiums are sent to all intending exhibitors. After the closing date for entries, passes, catalog numbers and schedules are sent to exhibitors. Points are awarded towards the Championship title by a judge who is approved by the Kennel Club. A total of fifteen points under three different judges must be gained for a dog to become a Champion, including two 'majors' under separate judges (3, 4, or 5 point wins). The size of the major is decided by the number of dogs entered at a show. The scale of Championship points is decided by the American Kennel Club, and this is calculated on the average number of Labradors shown in various regions of the USA. These are held annually or bi-annually by the club concerned, usually attracting large entries. Again, Championship points are awarded. The judge is normally someone held in high esteem by breeders and exhibitors, and sometimes an overseas judge receives an invitation to judge.

YOUR FIRST SHOW

It is a good idea to go as a spectator to your first few shows (minus your dog, as only dogs entered in the show are allowed in). Sit by the ringside and watch what the judge does with each dog, and how the dogs are expected to behave in the ring. You can then go home and practise with your dog, or you can go to the local ring training classes, where they will teach you all the basics.

It is a good idea to get used to ring procedures in this way, and for your dog to get used to being handled, before you attempt to compete in the ring. Judges expect dogs to behave well in the ring, although any judge worth their salt will forgive a puppy for being a bit playful. A dog must never show aggression in the ring, this is something that will not be tolerated, and you could find the judge asking you to leave the ring if this occurs.

When you are ready to attempt your first show, make sure you enter your puppy in a suitable class, according to his age. It is not a good idea to enter in too many classes at first, as both you and your dog should have a gentle introduction to the rigours of showing. Make sure you arrive at the showground in plenty of time so

ABOVE: Practice makes perfect, and this class of Labrador Retrievers know how to look their best for the judge.

LEFT: You must learn to move your dog at the correct pace to show the dog's gait and conformation to full advantage.

Show training can start from a very early age. These five-week-old puppies are already learning to stand in a show pose.

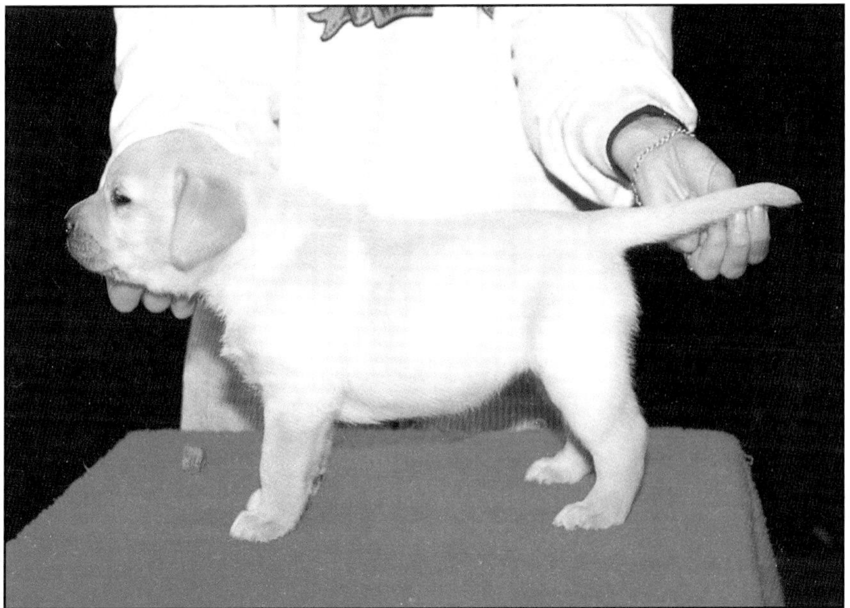

that you are not in a panic trying to find the ring where your class is being judged. Your dog should also be given a chance to acclimatise and get used to the unfamiliar environment. There are a few items of equipment you will need, and these should be packed in a show bag the day before the show. The bag must be large enough to carry a water-bowl, benching chains (UK only), collars, grooming gear, a show lead or leads, a towel, elementary first-aid items both for you and your dog, and a bag of tidbits to give your dog while he is being shown in the ring. At British shows a safety pin or a show-clip (which can be purchased at nearly all the dog-show stands) is essential. This is to pin on your number when you are in the ring. I also take along a small plastic bottle of drinking water. If the dog does not drink it all, it can come in handy for washing off mud or dirt, which your dog may have collected en route from the parking area to the ring.

PREPARING YOUR DOG

We are lucky that the Labrador Retriever is a short-coated breed, and there is little that needs to be done on the day of a show. Of course, your Labrador must be clean and sweet-smelling, and you may need to bath your dog before the show. If you do this, make sure you do not leave it until the last minute, as you will need a few days for the natural oils to return to the coat after bathing.

Nails should be trimmed, teeth should be clean, and the ears should be free from dirt or accumulated wax. Labradors are not trimmed for the show ring, with the exception of just tidying up the ragged hair at the end of the tail,using a pair of scissors. If you are not sure how to do this, wait until you get to the show and ask a more experienced exhibitor to show you what to do. Then all your Labrador will need is a good comb and brush, and perhaps a finish-off with one of the many patent grooming sprays available, and then you are ready for the ring. All dogs are shown on special show leads. This is basically a slender nylon slip-lead. Big collars and thick chunky leads are never used in the ring. The reason for this is that a slip-lead enables the exhibitor to loosen the lead, enabling the judge to see the dog's outline – the neck and shoulders – to full advantage. Show leads come in a variety of different colours, and the choice you make is a matter of personal preference.

RING PROCEDURE

Most judges follow a similar routine when judging a class. In each ring there is the appointed judge, and a steward whose job is to organise the entries according to the judge's instructions. The steward will call the dogs in for their allotted classes, and on entering the ring, all exhibitors will stand in a large circle with their dogs sideways on to the judge, who will be standing in the middle of the ring. After the judge has taken a quick look at the exhibits, you may all be asked to run round the ring so that the judge can have a look at toplines, tail carriage and sideways movement.

The judge will then move on to the individual examinations. The dog must stand steady while its mouth is checked to ensure it has the correct bite. The judge will then assess the head, checking eyes and eye-colour, expression, length and width of muzzle. Working down the dog, the judge will feel its neck down to the shoulders, go down the legs evaluating bone, look at the feet, and feel the body for length of couplings and rib cage to assess whether the dog is too fat or too thin, and then go over the hindquarters to feel for turn of stifle, width of loin etc. Finally, the judge will feel the coat to make sure it has the correct textured double coat, and ensure that the tail conforms to the required 'otter' tail, which is stipulated in the Breed Standard. You will then be asked to move your dog. Listen carefully as the judge will tell you how to move. It may be in a triangle, or straight up and down the ring, or both. If this is your first show, try to avoid being first in line for the individual examination. Give yourself a little time to watch the proceedings. Make sure you have enough room in the ring to show your dog off to its best advantage, but be respectful of dogs on either side of you. Try to avoid bunching up.

When you have been moved, the judge will allow you to go back to the side of the ring. The judge will look at all the dogs around the ring, and will pull out those that are short-listed. The others will be excused and can leave the ring. The judge will then place the dogs in order of merit.

BECOMING A JUDGE

BRITAIN

Right from the start, an aspiring judge is assessed by peers in the breed, rather than by a representative. After you have been exhibiting for a number of years, or better still, showing stock that you have bred and winning in good company, one of the more experienced breeders will suggest your name to a committee member of a canine society, recommending you be given a chance to judge at one of their shows – anything other than a Championship show.

If the committee agrees, you are the published judge. From then on it's up to you. Your peers will either enter under you, or just watch you. In order to be invited to judge at Championship show level, you need about five years open show judging, providing you have received good entries and you look as though you know what you are doing, and then one of the more experienced breeders will suggest your name to a society that is organising a Championship show. You are then sent a questionnaire by the Kennel Club, and you will have to list the dogs you have bred that have qualified with an entry in the KC Stud Book, and how long you have been judging the breed, at which shows, how many classes and your entries. These questionnaires are then sent to the breed clubs where they are voted upon, and the deciding vote is given by the Kennel Club. Providing you pass, you are still watched for a while and, if you do not draw enough entries, or have complaints made against you by either canine societies or exhibitors, then this privilege of being a recognised Championship Show judge can be taken away from you.

AMERICA

In the USA a prospective judge must have ten years experience in breeding and exhibiting; an applicant must have bred and raised four litters of any one breed, and produced two Champions from these litters. The applicant must have stewarding experience and must have judged at AKC sanctioned Matches, Sweepstakes or Futurities. The applicant who proceeds to the next stage must pass an examination on AKC rules, policies and judging procedures; pass a written test on the Breed Standard for each of the breeds applied for, and then must be interviewed in order to demonstrate breed knowledge and qualifications. Both in America and on the Continent aspiring judges go through a period where they are watched by a representative of their Kennel Club, and, depending on the representative's reports and the results of written exams, it is decided whether the applicant is ready and suitable to judge.

The sire and dam of a litter must be typical specimens of the breed and free from hereditary problems.

Chapter Six

BREEDING LABRADORS

TO BREED OR NOT TO BREED?

When you buy your first Labrador puppy, you probably have no thoughts of ever breeding a litter. However, as time goes on you may become more interested in this aspect of dog ownership. It could be that you enjoy your dog so much that you think it would be nice to have a son or daughter to carry on the family line. Or it could be that friends encourage you to breed a litter, as they want one of your bitch's puppies. Whatever the reason, this is not a step that should be undertaken lightly. It is a huge responsibility to bring new puppies into the world, and the cost, in terms

Good looks and sound temperament are equally important when you are breeding dogs.

of time and commitment, is impossible to assess. One final word of warning: never breed a litter because you think you will make some money. By the time you have taken all the expenses into account – the stud fee, possible veterinary fees, the cost of rearing the puppies, advertising the puppies for sale etc. – you are far more likely to make a loss.

ASSESSING YOUR BITCH

If, after due consideration, you are still keen to breed a litter, the first step is to ask a qualified person such as your bitch's breeder or a Championship show judge of your breed, to have a look at your bitch to see if she is good enough to be bred from. Physically, she must conform to the Breed Standard as closely as possible, and even more importantly, she must have a sound, equable temperament.

The next step is to have your bitch's eyes tested to see if she is clear of hereditary eye diseases. You will need to have her hips X-rayed, and she must achieve a satisfactory hip score before you proceed any further. (See Chapter 7.) Both of these tests should be carried out by a specialist; your vet will be able to recommend someone.

CHOOSING A STUD DOG

Once again, you should seek expert advice when it comes to choosing a stud dog. Your bitch's breeder will be able to tell you which lines tie in best with her pedigree, and you can also go to dog shows to discover the type of dog you like. Labradors are a wonderful breed, and one of the breed's greatest assets is temperament. You cannot place too much emphasis on ensuring that both dog and bitch have the sound, biddable character that is typical of the Labrador. You are also looking for a dog with a lovely noble head and good eye colour, giving that soft, gentle, mischievous expression. Good coats, and correctly made tails carried in the correct position complete the picture. The dog must also be sound, with good hips and free from any hereditary conditions. Breeders struggle for years to achieve all of these things, and even if you only intend to breed just one litter, you still do all you can to ensure that you try to produce sound, typical Labrador Retriever puppies.

THE MATING

When you have chosen a stud dog, you will need to make arrangements with the stud dog owner to plan the right day for the mating. I find it helpful if the bitch's owners telephone me on the first day of the season, and then we can work out the most likely day and make arrangements accordingly. The best time for mating is usually from the tenth to the thirteenth of the season, but some bitches vary. You must remember to keep your bitch away from other male dogs from the start of her season right through to the end – even after she has been mated.

Generally, a bitch is ready to be mated when the discharge from her vulva has changed colour from bright red to a clearer pinkish shade. Her vulva will be larger than usual and it will be be soft and pliable. When you touch your bitch on the top of her tail, she will turn it to one side. Beware though, bitches will sometimes do this for a day or two before they are ready to stand.

The stud dog will certainly tell you if you are too early, so be prepared to go back the next day or even the day after that. I would never take a maiden bitch (one that has never had a litter) to a stud dog that is owned by a complete novice. It is important to go to someone who knows what they are doing, and it certainly helps if you have an experienced stud dog who knows what is expected of him. You may be called on to hold your bitch steady during the mating, and if she is a maiden she may need encouragement and reassurance. The mating is followed by a phenomenon known as 'the tie'. The dog's enlarged penis is held by the constricting muscles of the vagina, and the dog will usually turn so that the dog and bitch are back to back. The tie varies in length from a few minutes to as long as forty-five minutes. During this time the dog and bitch must be held steady, as internal damage could result if they attempt to pull away from each other.

After the mating, it is customary to pay the stud fee, and you should receive a copy of the stud dog's pedigree plus the necessary Kennel Club paperwork for registering the litter. The fee you pay is for the mating itself, but if your bitch fails to come into whelp most breeders will offer a free repeat mating at a later date. This is not a requirement, but it is offered as a courtesy if you have used a proven stud dog.

THE PREGNANCY

A bitch's pregnancy lasts for approximately sixty-three days (nine weeks), and during this time she should continue to live a normal life just as she did prior to being mated. Do not increase her food until you are pretty sure that she is in whelp, which is usually any time after four weeks. You can make sure that your bitch definitely is in whelp by arranging for an ultrasound scan, and this will also tell you how many puppies the bitch is carrying. Alternatively, you can wait for the obvious signs of pregnancy – filling out behind and under the ribs, and the nipples getting pink and slightly larger.

The in-whelp bitch should be fed top-quality food, and she will need more protein, such as meat or eggs, or you can increase her all-in-one food. However, you do not want her to put on too much weight, as this can cause difficulties when it comes to whelping. Towards the end of her pregnancy, it is advisable to feed two meals a day, rather than one large one.

Your bitch will still need regular exercise, but do not allow her to jump about too much, or walk her too far from home. You will also need to introduce the bitch to her whelping quarters. If your bitch has always lived with you in the house, then this is where she will want to have her puppies, perhaps in a corner of the kitchen or in the utility room.

Wherever the whelping is to eventually take place, you will need a whelping box. The one I have is 4ft by 4ft (1.2m by 1.2m) with a marine ply floor. Three sides have boards 18ins high (46cms), and the front side is just 9ins high (23cms) with a facility to place another 9ins board on top at a later date. This is to keep the pups in when they first start to walk around. Make sure that the top board is easy to remove so that mum can get in and out easily without having to jump in blindly and risk landing on a puppy. The box should be lined with newspapers; you will need to collect stacks of newspapers ready for the whelping – they are wonderfully absorbent.

I always advise my vet that I have a bitch in whelp and tell him the due date, so that he is on standby in case of emergencies. If this is your first litter, you may want the vet to give your bitch a check-up, and this is a good time to ask for any advice. I would advise the novice to recruit a more experienced breeder to attend the whelping, if this is at all possible. A good many bitches whelp early, especially if they

The bitch should be kept fit during her pregnancy – and she should not become overweight as this will cause problems in whelping.

A bitch resting comfortably in her whelping box as she feeds her litter.

Both black and yellow puppies will be born in a litter when the sire and dam are different colours.

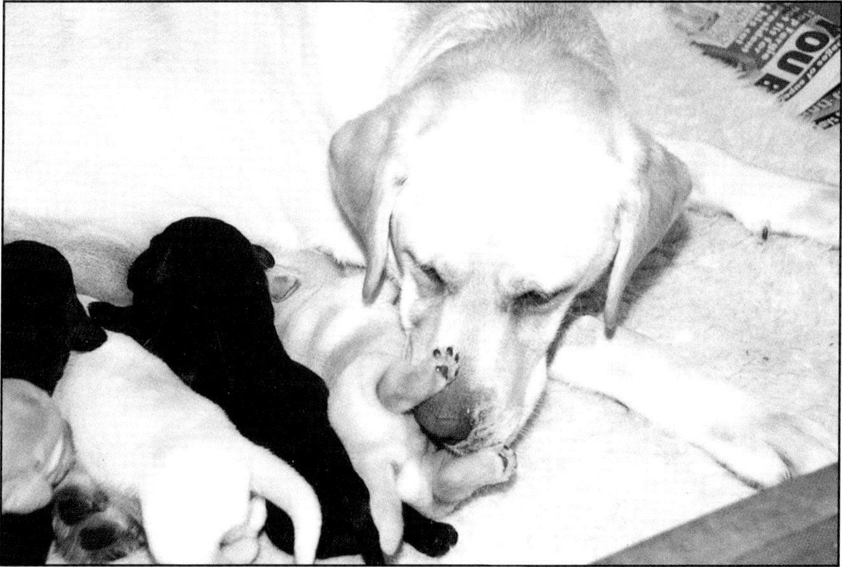

Labrador Retrievers generally make very good mothers and will clean and feed their puppies for the first few weeks.

are carrying a good-sized litter. Whelping up to five days early is nothing to be worried about. If the bitch whelps earlier than this, both the mother and the puppies will need extra care. If the bitch goes forty-eight hours beyond her due date, consult your vet.

THE WHELPING

It is usually quite obvious when a bitch is ready to start whelping. She will probably refuse food, and she will become increasingly restless. If she goes to her whelping box she will start tearing up the newspapers – preparing a nest for puppies. The bitch will probably want to urinate more often, and, if you take her temperature, you will find that it will have dropped from the normal 101 degrees Fahrenheit (38 degrees Centigrade) to 97 degrees Fahrenheit (35 degrees Centigrade). She will start to pant, this can go on all day, and as long as she shows no signs of distress, just allow things to progress normally. It goes without saying that you should keep other dogs, children and other distractions right away from her at this time.

As the labour moves into the second stage, she will start to have contractions as the puppy moves down the birth canal. Sometimes a little balloon will appear at the vulva entrance. Do not worry about this, it is just the forerunner of a puppy and is part of the fluid-filled membrane that the puppy is born in. After a few more heaves, the first puppy will emerge. Ninety-nine times out of a hundred your bitch will cope with everything herself. She will have the puppies effortlessly, she will sever the umbilical cord and clean up after each one.

However, you may have to step in and lend a hand. You must get the puppy out of the fluid-filled membrane as quickly as possible. Then you will need to clean the mucus and fluid away from the pup's nose, and cut the umbilical cord about two inches away from the pup. Give the pup a good rub with a towel until you can get it to squeal. Generally, the bitch will then take an interest, and you should encourage her to smell it and lick it, still holding the pup in the towel. Reassure your bitch the whole time, and tell her what a clever girl she has been. Hopefully, it will not be long before all the puppies have been born and are suckling contentedly.

It is important to keep the puppies warm; I have a heat lamp suspended over the whelping box. The ideal room temperature is between 75-80 degrees Fahrenheit (25 degrees Centigrade). It is a good idea to have a lined cardboard box with a covered hot-water bottle, and you can place the puppies in here when the bitch is in the process of giving birth.

During the whelping, I give my bitch small drinks of warm milk between deliveries. If, at any stage, your bitch is having contractions that go on for a long time with no result, contact your vet. This may occur during whelping, or before she has produced a pup. It may be that a puppy is presenting itself awkwardly, and the vet may be able to manipulate the puppy in the birth canal to present it the right way round for birth. It may be that a Caesarian is needed.

When whelping is complete, arrange with your vet to come and check your bitch to make sure she has delivered all the puppies and all the placentas. An antibiotic injection will help to combat any infections and help the uterus to contract. Your bitch will need a light meal after all the action, and then feed her as per usual but more often. I feed two milk meals and two meat meals the whole time the bitch is with her litter until I start to wean the puppies, then I reduce mum's intake.

REARING A LITTER

THE FIRST WEEK

For the first ten days or so the bitch will take care of all her puppies' needs, feeding them and cleaning up after them. You must ensure the bitch is comfortable, and make sure you keep the whelping room at constant temperature of 75-80 degrees Fahrenheit (25 degrees Centigrade). If you are using a heat lamp, make sure the bitch does not get over-heated if she is lying directly underneath it. A contented litter will be quiet and peaceful, with all the puppies feeding from their mother. If the puppies are huddled together and squeaking, they may be too cold, or there may be a problem with the bitch's milk supply.

The bitch should be getting plenty of good-quality food that is high in protein, and she should have fresh water available at all times. This should ensure a good milk supply. However, you should check the teats every day, and if one appears swollen and the puppies are avoiding it, apply a warm flannel and this will help to get the milk flowing again. Some breeders like to weigh the puppies at birth and then at intervals of three to four days to check they are going along nicely. Other breeders are quite happy to judge by appearance, and if the puppies are developing well and appear nicely-rounded they do not bother to get out the scales.

The bed must be kept scrupulously clean at all times. The best time to change the bedding is when the bitch goes out for a few minutes exercise. To begin with she may be very reluctant to leave her puppies. You may even have to use a lead and encourage her to come away. However, this situation will change, and increasingly, as the puppies grow older, she will appreciate a little time away from her puppies.

THE PUPPIES DEVELOP

By the time the puppies are ten days old their eyes will start to open. The ears develop from fourteen days, with hearing becoming acute by five weeks. The puppies will be standing upright by about three weeks and will be walking and running from four weeks. The stages of development are so rapid that it essential that you give the very best care during these vital weeks.

I start to wean the pups at three weeks of age, beginning with little balls of raw minced beef taken out of my hand. This is time-consuming if you have a large litter, but the pups are usually quick to get the idea. The puppies also have to learn to lap from a bowl – and this can be a very messy business. Eventually, I progress to feeding two milk meals and two meat meals (or a good all-in-one diet, given as directed) until the pups are eight weeks old and ready to go to their new homes.

From three weeks of age onwards you should trim the puppies' nails. These grow very quickly and it can be very painful for the mother if the pups scratch at her stomach as they are feeding. As soon as the puppies go on to solid food, the bitch will stop cleaning up after them – and so you must take over this chore. The bedding should be changed at regular intervals and you should pick up any mess immediately keeping the kennel area clean at all times. All puppies carry a roundworm burden, and you should worm the litter at five weeks and again at seven weeks. Your vet will supply a suitable treatment. A worming paste is available, and this is probably the easiest to administer.

The puppies will start playing with each other between three and four weeks, and it is ideal if you can put them in a play-pen where they have the space to move

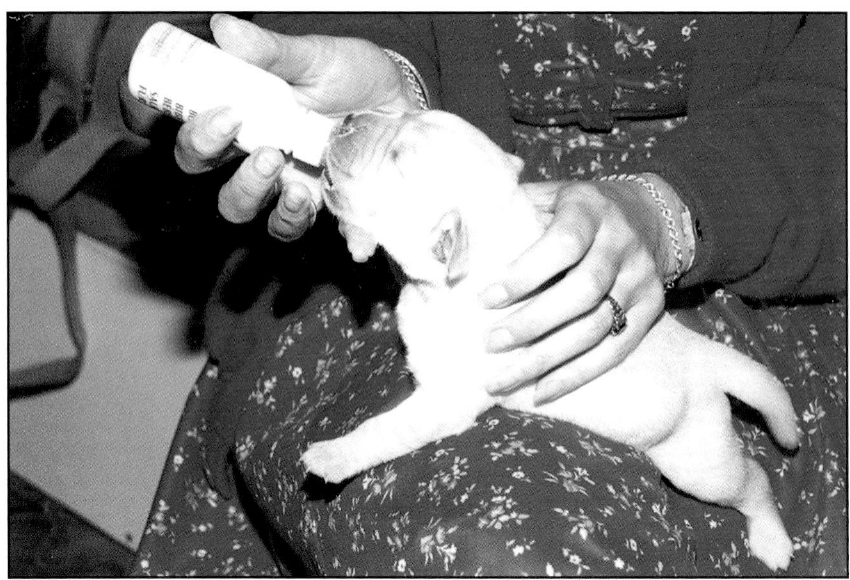

If the bitch has a large litter, you may need to help her out by bottle-feeding the puppies.

An evenly-matched litter, ready to start exploring the outside world.

By five weeks of age the puppies should be sturdy, and nicely covered rather than overweight.

Good feeding is the essence of successful rearing, and these puppies are now ready to go off to their new homes.

around, but they are safe and secure. On warm days the play-pen can be put in the garden, and the puppies will benefit from the fresh air and the sunshine. You can supply some safe toys for them to play with. You do not have to spend money on these – the puppies will get hours of fun from playing with a cardboard box. This is probably the most fascinating time of all: watching the puppies playing together, interacting with each other, and seeing how their characters develop. All breeders agree this is the most time-consuming part of rearing a litter! Obviously, you will need to find out as much information as you can before breeding a litter, and there are many books which deal with the subject in greater detail. Hopefully, you now have some idea of what is involved, and if you wish to proceed further, I can assure you that despite all the hard work involved, there is nothing more rewarding than breeding and rearing a healthy litter of Labrador puppies.

Chapter Seven

HEALTH CARE

Labrador Retrievers are an active, healthy breed; they are easy to care for, and, hopefully, your visits to the vet will be few and far between. However, all dogs are likely to suffer from some ailment or have a minor accident at some point in their lives, and it is advisable to acquire some basic knowledge so that you can assess your dog's condition and administer basic treatments.

FINDING A VET

The vet is a key figure in your dog's life, and I would advise that right from the start, when you take your pup for his first inoculation, you find a vet that you can feel at ease with. You want someone who will take the time to explain everything to you: what is wrong with your dog, the type of medication prescribed, possible side-effects, and roughly how long the condition will take to clear up.

It is also important to watch how the vet gets on with your Labrador. Vets do vary, and just like doctors, some have a good "bedside manner", while others like to surround their profession with an air of mystique. Try to find a veterinary practice that has twenty-four hour cover. A dog can become ill in the middle of the night – and you can age a hundred years trying to get professional help in the small hours.

The golden rule when caring for your Labrador is, if in doubt, call your vet. If a dog is taken to the vet in the early stages of an illness, this can not only save the dog from suffering a lot of discomfort, it can also save you a lot of worry. It may also save you money, as treatment obviously becomes more complicated when a condition has reached an advanced stage. A good vet is like a good family doctor, and it is well worth the search to find the best in your area.

FIRST AID

There are a number of minor ailments or injuries that you can cope with in the home, and it is advisable to have a small first aid kit so you are equipped to deal with the more common problems. I suggest you keep in stock:

Cotton-wool (cotton).
Bandages (cotton and crepe).
A roll of inch wide adhesive tape (for fastening a bandage).
A mild disinfectant (suitable for washing cuts etc.).
Ear-drops.
A box of cotton buds.
A bottle of hydrogen peroxide (for treatment of eczema).

If you ever have any doubts about your dog's health, the golden rule is to consult your vet.

Your responsibility lasts for your dog's lifetime, and as your dog gets older, you must tailor diet and exercise to suit the individual's needs.

The aim of every dog owner is to have a happy, healthy, well-cared-for animal.

A bottle of liquid paraffin (for treatment of constipation).
A treatment for diarrhoea (ask your vet for advice).
A thermometer.
A bottle of cough medicine.
Antiseptic powder.
Antiseptic cream.
A pair of scissors
A pair of tweezers.

COMMON PROBLEMS

COUGHS

Coughs can have many causes. The most distressing and contagious is Kennel Cough, which can be caught by all dogs, not just those that are confined to kennels. The signs are a very dry, husky cough, which is very distressing. This is a contagious disease that has to take its course, and all you can do is relieve the symptoms. Most dogs respond well to a dose of cough medicine, and the type used to treat adult humans is perfectly safe. It is essential that you keep your dog at home and avoid all contact with other dogs, until you are confident that your dog has completely recovered. There is a vaccination against kennel cough which is quite effective. This is not a life-threatening condition, but old dogs and puppies are obviously more at risk. Coughing can also be a sign of worm infestation, and in rare cases, it may be the first sign of heart disease. If your dog is getting on in years and is coughing, you would be wise to ask your vet for advice.

CUTS

Minor cuts should be cleaned with antiseptic and then left to heal. Dogs usually lick a wound clean, and provided the dog does not keep on licking to excess, this usually helps the cut to heal. If the cut is more serious, it may be better to cover it with a bandage, providing the cut is located on a part of the body that can be easily bandaged. Make sure that the bandage is not too tight, and remember to fasten it with adhesive tape, and not a safety-pin.

If your dog has a really deep cut, stitches will probably be required. You will need to put a temporary bandage on the wound, and then go to the vet as soon as possible, first telephoning so that the vet knows what to expect. If the vet decides to come to your house, try to keep the dog as quiet as possible and, if you can, hold the edges of the cut together.

After the wound has been stitched, it is important to make sure that the dog does not worry at the stitches. If this happens, the vet may suggest that your dog wears a plastic collar – sometimes known as an Elizabethan collar. It looks rather like a lampshade, with the smaller end attached to a collar around the dog's neck. It does not look very comfortable, but it does stop your dog from reaching the wound, and, in fact, most dogs adapt surprisingly quickly to the Elizabethan 'frill'.

EARS

Ears need checking regularly in order to keep them clean and sweet-smelling. When ears get dirty and wax builds up they can be prone to infection. If your Labrador keeps shaking his head, or one ear hangs down lower than the other, there is probably a problem. Labradors love swimming, but when your dog comes out of the water make sure you dry his ears. You only need to dry the external part of the ear – never poke anything into the ear.

Sometimes you will find a black deposit in the ears. This might be just where the dog has got very hot and collected dirt around the ear, or it could be caused by ear mites. Use a few drops of your ear cleaner, drop them into the ear and gently massage it. Leave for a few seconds then wipe away any deposit from the outer ear with a cotton bud or cotton-wool. If, after a few days of treatment, the dog is still uncomfortable, then take him to the vet.

ECZEMA

This starts with a wet patch appearing on the skin, usually as a result of the dog getting overheated, or nibbling itself due to an allergic reaction. It can also result from fleas. The most effective treatment is to cut the hair from around the affected area, and dab with either hydrogen peroxide or an antisepetic solution. The wet patch should soon dry up without spreading any further, and the hair will slowly grow to cover the place.

If either of these remedies fail to have the desired effect and the wet patch increases in size, then ask your vet for advice.

EYES

If your Labrador gets runny eyes, especially in the summer, this can be caused by dust. Some dogs also suffer from a form of hay-fever. Bathing the eyes with cold tea (no milk or sugar!) or a patent eye-wash, will remedy this. If your dog has matter in the eyes, or constantly runny eyes that seem irritated, ask your vet for advice. This could be a symptom of a more serious problem, particularly if your dog appears to be off-colour, so professional advice should be sought.

Constantly running eyes can be caused by a condition called Entropion. This is where the eyelid rolls inward and the eyelashes come into contact with the eye-ball. This, if not treated, is very uncomfortable, and in severe cases it could cause blindness. Your vet will advise you if this is the case and will recommend surgery. It is a simple operation leaving the tiniest of scars, which soon becomes covered with hair. As this is, or can be, an hereditary defect, the dog should not be used for breeding.

FLEAS

Some dogs are allergic to fleas, and will keep on worrying and scratching at the flea bites. The trick is to stop this before the bites turn into eczema patches. The best method is to use an aerosol spray with a patent flea-killer, making sure you follow the manufacturers' instructions.

LAMENESS

There can be many reasons for a dog becoming lame, but it is always worth checking the feet to start with. It could well be that a thorn or a sharp stone has got stuck in the pad. This is where your tweezers come in handy. After removing the foreign object, dab the affected spot with a little antiseptic, and there should be no further problems. Sometimes a dog will cut its pad and a stitch may be required, or it may break a nail. In both these cases, make sure you keep the wound site clean, and

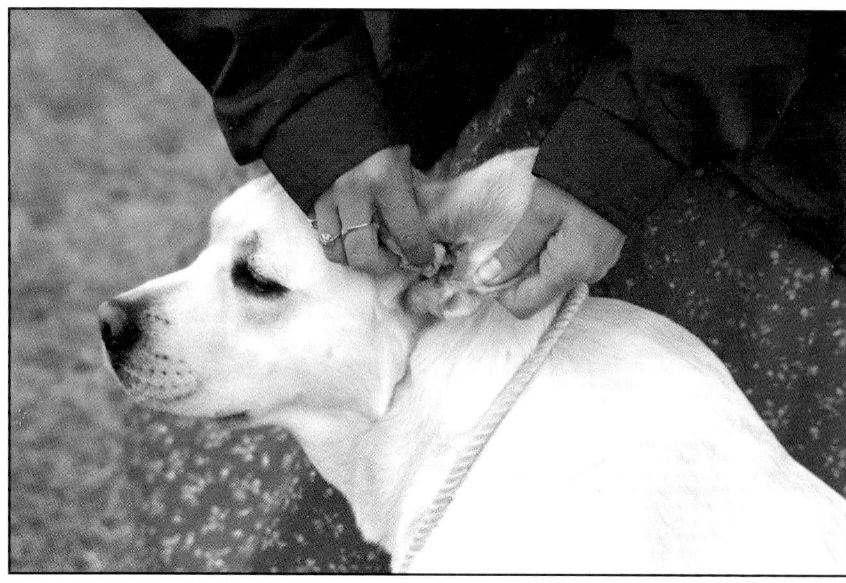

Ears should be clean and sweet-smelling, but take care not to probe too deeply.

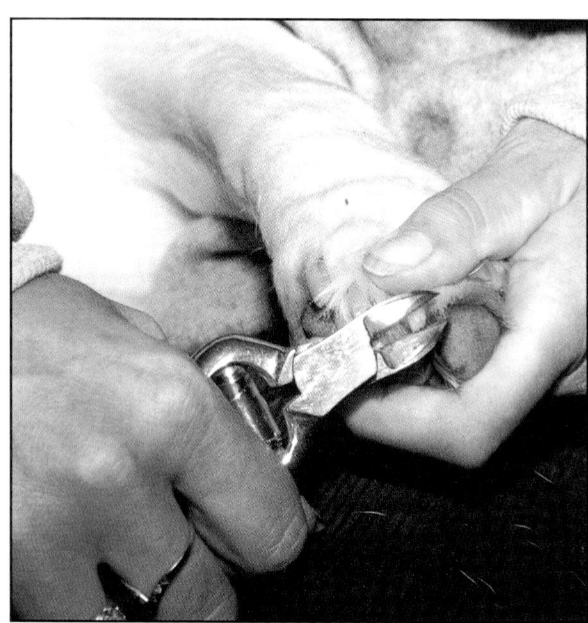

Nails should not be allowed to grow too long, and they may need to be trimmed with nail-clippers.

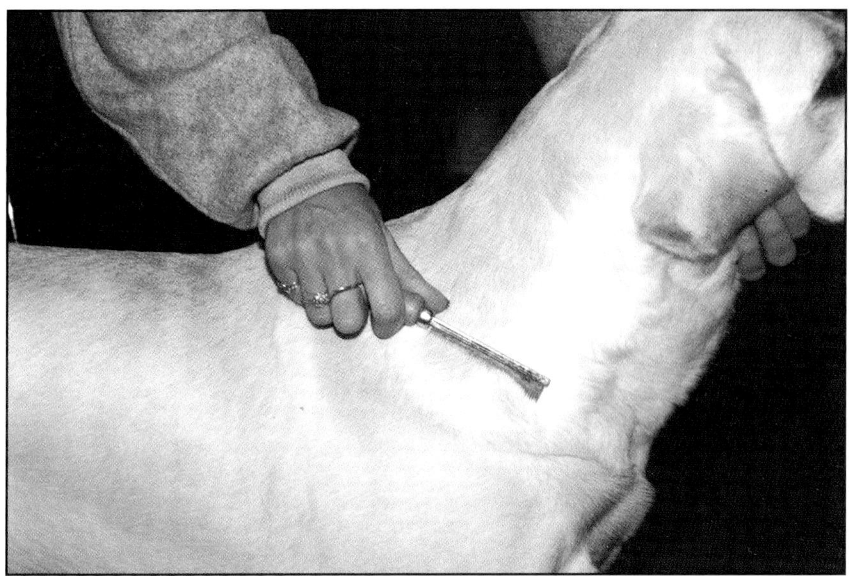

The short-coated Labrador Retriever is easy to care for, and a regular weekly grooming session will keep the coat in good condition.

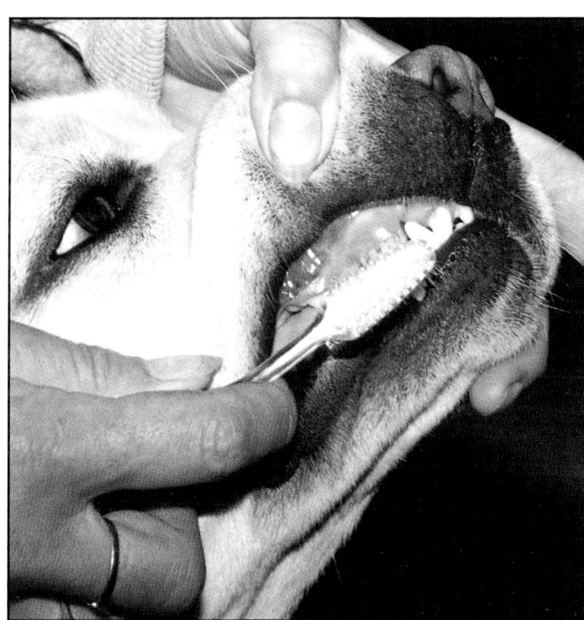

If your dog's teeth start to collect tartar they should be cleaned with a toothbrush, using canine toothpaste.

keep a close check until it has completely healed. If you can find nothing wrong with the feet and your dog is still lame, it could mean that he has a sprain. Feel for any heat in the leg, and then bathe in alternate hot and cold water. Try to make the dog rest as much as possible. If the lameness persists, consult your vet.

STOMACH UPSETS

If you suspect your Labrador has swallowed something that is likely to disagree with it, such as a handkerchief, a sock, a small stone or similar object, a dose of liquid paraffin will help the article to work its way through. You can give two or three doses, but if you get no results or your dog goes off its food or looks bloated i.e. its stomach starts to swell, and it is visibly distressed, then you will need professional advice. However, liquid paraffin usually does the trick. I have recovered two nylon slip leads, a handkerchief and a linen table napkin using this method! It is also a useful remedy if your dog appears to be suffering from constipation.

If, on the other hand, your dog has diarrhoea, you will need to give a dose of medicine, recommended by your vet, and starve your dog for twenty-four hours. Make sure there is plenty of clean drinking water available at all times, as it is important that the dog does not get dehydrated This is a condition that must not be ignored, and if it goes on for a day or two without signs of improvement, call your vet. If you see signs of blood in the motions, you should contact your vet immediately.

TEMPERATURE

There are many reasons why a dog may develop a temperature, and if your dog is off-colour, it may be useful to take his temperature to help assess the overall condition. This is done by inserting your thermometer one to one and a half inches into the dog's anal canal, using a twisting motion. This can be facilitated if you apply a little Vaseline to the end of the thermometer. Hold it in place for two to three minutes, making sure you hold the dog steady, and then gently withdraw it. The average temperature for an adult dog is 101.5 degrees Fahrenheit.

WORMS

ROUNDWORM: This is the most common type of worms, and most dogs will have an infestation at some time in their lives, particularly in the first twelve months of life. When you buy your puppy, it should have been wormed for roundworm, and you should be given details of the worming programme, and when the next treatment is due. I usually suggest that all dogs are wormed at six-monthly intervals.

If you suspect that your dog has worms, the signs to look for are loss of condition, with a dry 'starey' coat i.e. the coat does not lie down in a sleek fashion; it stands up slightly from the skin, and it lacks the gloss that a good coat should have. Bad breath, a voracious appetite and a pot-belly can also indicate worm infestation. Strangely, loss of appetite can also be a sign that worms may be present.

Worm tablets can be bought from any pet shop, or your vet will supply them. Use as directed, and do not be tempted to "throw an extra one in for luck", as this could do more harm than good. Some worming preparations will actually melt the worms and you will see no signs of them in the dog's motions, others will dislodge the worms and they will be seen in the motions.

TAPEWORM: If you live and exercise your dog in sheep country, you run the risk of your dog contracting tapeworms, especially if you run your dog over sheep pastures. Even the most well brought up dog seems to be unable to resist eating sheep droppings from time to time, and this results in tapeworm infestation.

These are a little more difficult to dislodge than the roundworms because they actually hook themselves on to the intestine and grow from there. They are a segmented parasite, and this can actually prove to be their undoing, as segments tend to break off and pass through, very often remaining around the dog's anus. If you see small square-looking segments in that area, accompanied by poor condition, bad breath, etc. then ask your vet to prescribe a tapeworm treatment.

HEREDITARY DISEASES

Like most other breeds, the Labrador Retriever does have a few hereditary diseases. It is important to be aware of these, particularly if you have plans to breed your dog.

EYES

ENTROPION: Fortunately, this condition, where the eyelids turn inwards, is becoming increasingly rare as most breeders have stopped breeding from affected stock. However, it can appear out of the blue. Surgery is straightforward and effective.

PROGRESSIVE RETINAL ATROPHY (PRA): All responsible breeders have their breeding stock checked annually by an authorised vet for this disease. As the name implies, it is an atrophying of the retina. This can take quite a while to develop, and some dogs may be seven years old or even older before the condition becomes apparent to the owner, although it may also appear at an earlier age. If you plan to use your dog for breeding, it is advisable to have the eyes checked as soon as it is old enough (i.e. twelve months), and then on an annual basis thereafter. This condition results in blindness, and so all preventative measures must be taken to reduce its incidence.

HIP DYSPLASIA

This condition affects the ball and socket joint of the hind legs, and it is more likely to appear in the larger and heavier breeds. A dog can be born with seemingly normal hips, and it is only when it matures that the problem becomes apparent. The only way to detect hip dysplasia is by X-ray, and unless you intend to breed with your dog, or you suspect there is a problem, there is no need to have your dog X-rayed. The earliest age that you can have your dog X-rayed for hip dysplasia is twelve months (twenty-four months in the USA), and the results are then scored. The degree of dysplasia can vary widely, and some dysplastic dogs are never lame in their lifetime. However, responsible breeders try to breed from relatively sound stock, and in this way, the number of dogs suffering from this condition is greatly reduced. Dogs suffering from severe hip dysplasia can undergo surgery.

OSTEOCHONDROSIS

There is evidence to suggest this is an inherited condition, although other factors

Once you have owned a Labrador Retriever, you will never want to be without one.

such as injury, excessive exercise and over-supplementation of additives to the diet are contributory. It usually occurs in the larger fast-growing breeds, and develops between four and twelve months of age. The problem occurs when cartilage flakes off from the bone, and this may occur in the shoulder, hocks or stifles. The signs are gradual lameness. Rest may solve the problem, but surgery is the only solution in more severe cases. This is most successful when it is the shoulder that is affected.